A HANDBOOK FOR
SUBSTITUTE TEACHERS

A HANDBOOK FOR
SUBSTITUTE TEACHERS

By

ANNE WESCOTT DODD

CHARLES C THOMAS • PUBLISHER
Springfield • Illinois • U.S.A.

Published and Distributed Throughout the World by
CHARLES C THOMAS • PUBLISHER
2600 South First Street
Springfield, Illinois 62794-9265

© *1989 by* CHARLES C THOMAS • PUBLISHER

ISBN 0-398-05539-4

Library of Congress Catalog Card Number: 88-24905

With THOMAS BOOKS *careful attention is given to all details of manufacturing and design. It is the Publisher's desire to present books that are satisfactory as to their physical qualities and artistic possibilities and appropriate for their particular use.* THOMAS BOOKS *will be true to those laws of quality that assure a good name and good will.*

Printed in the United States of America
Q-R-3

Library of Congress Cataloging in Publication Data

Dodd, Anne W.
    A handbook for substitute teachers / by Anne Wescott Dodd.
      p. cm.
    Bibliography: p.
    Includes index.
    ISBN 0-398-05539-4
    1. Substitute teachers — United States — Handbooks, manuals, etc. I. Title.
LB2844.1.S8D63 1989
371.1′4122′0973 — dc19   88-24905
                                                            CIP

For . . . .
KISA, TASHKA, AND AGASSIZ

PREFACE

MY OWN CAREER as a substitute teacher was very brief but long enough so that even after many years, I still clearly recall how frightening it was to walk into a strange school and face a sea of unfamiliar faces. Since one of my favorite games as a difficult-to-manage elementary and high school student had been, "Get the Sub," I just knew these students, no matter how quiet and well-behaved they appeared, were plotting and planning ways to do me in. I mentally prepared myself for the mischief that would surely follow.

Fortunately most students had better things to think about--parties, girl friends, boy friends, games after school--so the classroom situations my imagination conjured up were far worse than those that ever occurred.

Being prepared for any contingency though is the only way to make it successfully as a sub. Every sub needs a survival kit, and that's what I hope this book will be: a resource to which substitute teachers (and regular teachers) can go to find answers, advice, and teaching ideas.

Most of what's in the book comes from my own experiences over many years in schools at all levels as a substitute teacher, regular teacher, principal, and teacher educator, but others have contributed as well. I'd like to recognize and thank my former students; participants in my substitute teacher workshop; the many substitute teachers with whom I've come in contact; Eileen Landay and other members of the Freeport teachers' writing group; teachers Linda Smith and Carla Rensenbrink; teacher and writer Richard Lederer; and finally my husband, Jim, loyal supporter, critic, and proofreader.

CONTENTS

A HANDBOOK FOR
SUBSTITUTE TEACHERS

PART ONE

Chapter One

IS SUBSTITUTE TEACHING
A JOB FOR YOU?

KAREN quit college after completing only two years. Now that both her children are in school, she wants a job that will allow her to be home when they are and to take time off when one of them is sick or there's a special event at school.

Walt was forced to retire early from a middle management position in a large company. He'd like to do something different, but he also wants a couple of months free to go to Florida in the winter and time to garden and fish in the summer.

Lucille, whose husband has just transferred for the third time in five years, is new in town. She doesn't have any idea how long they'll be here and she wishes she could find something she could do no matter where she lives.

Jackie graduates from college mid-year and discovers she must wait until fall for a regular teaching position to open up. Meanwhile she knows her night job at a restaurant won't help her get hired as a teacher.

Substitute teaching may be the perfect job for these people and for you if you're looking for interesting and flexible part-time work.

You may be surprised to learn that common sense and the ability to get along with children are more important for substitute teachers than teacher training. If you like children and have some experience with them--as a parent, church school teacher, coach, or youth group leader-- you should consider substitute teaching.

3

ARE YOU QUALIFIED?

In most states substitute teachers do not have to be trained as teachers. In fact, only a few states (Colorado, Iowa, Michigan, Minnesota, Nebraska, North Dakota, Oregon, Pennsylvania, Rhode Island, Texas, Washington, and Wisconsin) require that subs meet the same standards as regular teachers, and even in these states the standards may be relaxed somewhat when the shortage of subs makes that necessary. Many states have no minimum requirements--a high school diploma is all that's needed in South Dakota--and several others allow substitutes to teach without a college degree.

What this all means is that even though you are not a college graduate and never took an education course, you may qualify to be a substitute teacher in your area. Check the chart for general information or, if you want more specifics, contact your state department of education [A list appears in the appendix.] or the office of your local superintendent of schools. Individual districts may set higher standards than the state minimum, but even these are often waived when enough fully qualified subs cannot be found to meet the demand.

Figure 1

REQUIREMENTS FOR SUBSTITUTE TEACHERS BY STATE

	Minimum Education	*Full Certification?*	*Exam?*
ALABAMA	Local Requirements	No	No
ALASKA	High school grad	No	No
ARIZONA	College grad	No	No
ARKANSAS	None	No	No
CALIFORNIA	College grad	No	Yes
COLORADO	*College grad/tchr. prep	Yes	Yes
CONNECTICUT	College grad	No	No
DELAWARE	Some college	No	No
WASHINGTON, D.C.	60 credit hours	No	No
FLORIDA	High school grad	No	No
GEORGIA	High school grad	No	No
HAWAII	High school grad	No	No
IDAHO	Local requirements	No	No
ILLINOIS	College grad	No	No
INDIANA	60 credit hours	No	No
IOWA	College grad/tchr. prep	Yes	No
KANSAS	Two years college	No	No
KENTUCKY	*64 credit hours	No	No
LOUISIANA	Local requirements	No	No
MAINE	High school grad	No	No

Figure 1 *(Continued)*

	Minimum Education	Full Certification?	Exam?
MARYLAND	Local requirements	No	No
MASSACHUSETTS	Local requirements	No	No
MICHIGAN	*College grad/tchr. prep	Yes	No
MINNESOTA	College grad/tchr. prep	Yes	Yes
MISSISSIPPI	Local requirements	No	No
MISSOURI	Two years college	No	No
MONTANA	High school grad	No	No
NEBRASKA	College grad/tchr. prep	Yes	No
NEVADA	62 credit hours/6 ed.	No	No
NEW HAMPSHIRE	Local requirements	No	No
NEW JERSEY	Two years college	No	No
NEW MEXICO	High school grad	No	No
NEW YORK	High school grad	No	No
NORTH CAROLINA	*College grad	No	No
NORTH DAKOTA	College grad/tchr. prep	Yes	No
OHIO	College grad	No	No
OKLAHOMA	None for under 35 days	No (Yes for 35 +)	No
OREGON	College grad/tchr. prep	Yes	Yes
PENNSYLVANIA	College grad/tchr. prep	Yes	Yes
RHODE ISLAND	College grad/tchr. prep	Yes	No
SOUTH CAROLINA	Local requirements	No	No
SOUTH DAKOTA	High school grad	No	No
TENNESSEE	High school grad	No	No
TEXAS	*College grad/tchr. prep	Yes	No
UTAH	High school grad	No	No
VERMONT	High school grad	No	No
VIRGINIA	*College grad/tchr. prep	Yes (60 + days/yr.)	Yes
WASHINGTON	College grad/tchr. prep	Yes	No
WEST VIRGINIA	College grad	No	No
WISCONSIN	College grad/tchr. prep	Yes	No
WYOMING	Two years college	No	No

*Someone who does not meet all the requirements may be eligible to teach if no fully qualified substitute teachers are available or for a limited number of days per year.

And there is a great demand everywhere. A few years ago a study revealed that over 4 percent of the nation's teachers were absent on an average day. Today that figure is higher. Because of recent efforts to reform education, teachers are often released from their regular duties to visit other teachers' classes, attend workshops, and develop curriculum. Because of the increased need, some schools employ permanent subs who, if they are not needed to cover classes, help out around the school in other ways.

School districts, both large and small, are unable to find enough subs. San Diego schools were short 20-50 teachers per week while a small school in the Midwest had to close for two days when five of its twenty teachers came down with the flu. According to testimony for a school finance suit in New Jersey, Paterson had 120 teachers absent while the district could find only 8-10 substitute teachers.

The chart indicates the demand for substitutes in each state as reported by officials in the state departments of education. In some cases they may underestimate the need for subs because they are not familiar with problems at the local level. I have yet to meet a principal anywhere in the country who has enough substitute teachers to call on.

WHAT'S THE PAY?

Substitute pay varies from district to district, and while no one will ever get rich as a substitute teacher, the pay for six hours or less of work per day is well above the minimum wage. You can expect anywhere from $20-50 a day in rural areas to $80 or more in some urban and suburban districts. Los Angeles increased its daily pay to $120 for teachers willing to sub in inner-city schools. General information for each state is summarized in the chart.

Figure 2

ESTIMATED DAILY PAY AND EMPLOYMENT OPPORTUNITIES
IN EACH STATE

	Day-To-Day	*Long-Term*	*Supply**
ALABAMA	Below $30	per diem/schedule	N/A
ALASKA	$50 - 75	$50 - 75	about right
ARIZONA	$30 - 50	$30 - 50	
rural			not enough
suburbs			too many
ARKANSAS	$30 - 50	$30 - 50	about right
CALIFORNIA	$50 - 75	$75 - 100	about right
COLORADO	varies by district		N/A
CONNECTICUT	$30 - 50	$30 - 50	not enough
DELAWARE	$30 - 50	$30 - 50	about right
WASHINGTON, D.C.	$30 - 50	$50 - 75	about right
FLORIDA	varies by district		N/A
GEORGIA	$30 - 75	$30 - 75	not enough
HAWAII	$75 - 100	$75 - 100	not enough
IDAHO	N/A		about right
ILLINOIS	$30 - 50	$30 - 50	about right
INDIANA	$30 - 50	$30 - 50 (more if cert.)	not enough
IOWA	$30 - 50	$30 - 50	not enough
KANSAS	$30 - 50	$50 - 75	about right
KENTUCKY	varies by district		N/A

Figure 2 *(Continued)*

	Day-To-Day	Long-Term	Supply*
LOUISIANA	$30 - 50	$30 - 50	not enough
MAINE	$30 - 50	per diem/schedule	not enough
MARYLAND	$30 - 50	$30 - 50	about right
MASSACHUSETTS	$30 - 50	$30 - 50	not enough
MICHIGAN	$30 - 75	$30 - 75	not enough
MINNESOTA	N/A		about right
MISSISSIPPI	Below $30	$30 - 50	not enough
MISSOURI	$30 - 50	$30 - 50	about right
MONTANA	$50 - 75	must be certified	about right
NEBRASKA	$50 - 75	$50 - 75	about right
NEVADA	$30 - 50	$30 - 50	depends on area
NEW HAMPSHIRE	$30 - 50	$30 - 50	not enough
NEW JERSEY	N/A		about right
NEW MEXICO	varies by district		about right
NEW YORK	$30 - 50	$30 - 50	not enough
NORTH CAROLINA	$30 - 50	$30 - 50	about right
NORTH DAKOTA	$30 - 50	$30 - 50	about right
OHIO	$50 - 75	per diem/schedule	not enough
OKLAHOMA	$30 - 50	$30 - 50	about right
OREGON	$75 - 100	$75 - 100 +	about right
PENNSYLVANIA	$30 - 50	$50 - 75	not enough
RHODE ISLAND	$30 - 50	$50 - 75	not enough
SOUTH CAROLINA	varies by district		N/A
SOUTH DAKOTA	$30 - 50	$30 - 50	too many
TENNESSEE	$30 - 50	per diem/schedule	about right
TEXAS	$30 - 50	$30 - 50	not enough
UTAH	$30 - 50	$30 - 50	about right
VERMONT	$50 - 75	$50 - 75	about right
VIRGINIA	varies by district		N/A
WASHINGTON	$50 - 75	per diem/schedule	not enough
WEST VIRGINIA	$50 - 75	$75 - 100	not enough
WISCONSIN	N/A		about right
WYOMING	$30 - 50	$50 - 75	varies by district

*Estimates are from state departments of education and may not accurately reflect the supply of substitutes in a given district. In some states long-term substitutes must be certified and thus will be paid at the same rate as regular teachers in the district.

As a day-to-day sub, you are not usually entitled to any fringe benefits, but neither do you have to make any long-term commitment. You can put your name on the sub list and take it off at any time during the school year. Long-term subs, those who fill in for regular teachers on maternity or extended sick leave, are paid more, often at the same rate as regular teachers, but these positions are rarely filled by anyone who does not have a valid teaching certificate.

Again, the office of the superintendent of schools is the place to ask about pay and also what the procedure is for getting hired. In some cases all you'll have to do to get your name on the day-to-day substitute list is fill out an application. In others you may also have to interview with the superintendent, or personnel officer, or principal. Long-term subs are usually hired in the same manner as regular teachers. You'll find detailed information on getting hired in Chapter Three.

ADVANTAGES AND DISADVANTAGES

Because school ends by 2 or 3 P.M., you can substitute and still have time to look for a permanent job. Substituting can also be combined with parttime evening or weekend work or study. You can take a day off whenever you need or want to (although the reason to give when you refuse any job is that you're unavailable).

Substituting is one of the best ways to land a regular teaching or paraprofessional position since you can meet the people who count, find out which schools and students you like best, and gain valuable experience that will help you avoid many of the mistakes beginning teachers make early on and have to live with until June. A student teacher who graduated in May and is fully qualified to teach plans instead to substitute next fall. She wants to check out all the schools in the area where she'll be living to find out where she would prefer to teach on a permanent basis.

Finally you can substitute wherever you are and wherever you go. If you have to move every year or two because a spouse gets transferred by his or her company, you're married to someone in the military, or you'd just like to try living in different parts of the country before you settle down, you'll be able to find employment as a substitute teacher wherever you land. The skills you gain in one place will make you more successful in other places because schools aren't all that different.

But if you're a substitute, you can't count on a regular paycheck. Some weeks you'll work every day, but there'll be others when you're needed only for a day or two. Because you won't always know ahead of time when you're going to work, you'll have to cope with calls at 6 A.M. as well as adapt to teaching different age groups and subjects on short notice.

Despite the drawbacks, however, substituting is never boring. Working with young people is a great way to stay young, to keep in touch with what's going on, and, if you're a parent, to become more effective in handling your own children.

BUT WHAT ABOUT DISCIPLINE?

Sounds good, you say, but... You've heard some real horror stories about how tough kids are these days, and you remember what a hard time you gave subs when you were in school. If you are firm, fair, and friendly, you can handle most kids in most classrooms. Remember, news stories document the extremes. Of course, the students will test you at first, but you'll pass the test by not losing your cool or your self-confidence. One sub, a young woman who looks no older than her students, advises, "Be confident! Don't let the kids know if you are scared or nervous. Take charge of the situation even if you have to fake it!" This method worked for her even with a notorious class of eighth graders, generally considered to be the most difficult age group anyway. Chapter Five provides tips for successful subbing.

Substitute teaching is like anything else. The more you do it, the better you'll get. But first you have to plunge right in and get your feet wet. Go ahead. What have you got to lose? You may even find you like teaching well enough to want to do it fulltime. If so, your timing is right: a growing teacher shortage has replaced the glut of a few years ago. Good teachers like good subs won't have any trouble finding jobs. This book will help you become a successful substitute teacher.

Chapter Two

WHAT SCHOOLS AND STUDENTS ARE
RIGHT FOR YOU?

SUCCESSFUL substitute teachers enjoy working with people, especially children and teenagers. They welcome challenges. They
don't mind doing things on short notice and like variety more than
routines. They can make good decisions without the luxury of time to
plan everything ahead. They're self confident, resilient, and optimis-
tic. They have plenty of good old-fashioned common sense and a
sense of humor.

Especially in the elementary school, some successful subs are good
entertainers. They can hold the attention of students with story-
telling, songs, or theater games. Others are good at working with arts
and crafts or directing sports and games, but most successful subs are
just ordinary people with no special talent except a sincere interest in
young people and in creating an environment where students feel that
they are trusted and cared for as they participate in meaningful learning activities.

Good substitutes, like good teachers, are not demanding task masters
or drill sergeants nor are they overly friendly or so willing to please that
anything goes. Good subs are firm, fair, and friendly. They believe in
themselves and in their students. The students sense their honest concern and commitment and usually respond in kind.

Because children change as they grow older and because schools and
teachers reflect differing philosophies of education, substitutes will face
different challenges and reap different benefits depending upon the age
group and the particular classroom and school in which they work.
You'll have to decide what schools and students are best for you.

PHILOSOPHICAL CONSIDERATIONS

In general, schools in the United States fall into three categories: elementary, middle school/junior high, and senior high schools. The grades, kindergarten through grade twelve, may be structured differently in your community than in a neighboring one, but the categories described later in this chapter will be useful for you to judge which level or levels would be best for you.

Schools and classrooms also differ because of differences in the basic philosophical ideas on which their programs are based. The following descriptions of three types of approaches are not definitive, but they will help you to make a general assessment about a particular school or classroom. You'll be more comfortable teaching in a school or classroom which most closely reflects your own beliefs about education.

The Traditional Approach

Traditional schools haven't changed much over the years. Because they are conservative, they tend to adopt new ideas very slowly, if at all. They usually have fairly rigid rules and procedures, place heavy emphasis on the three R's, and maintain very tight discipline. Here are some things you'll probably notice in this type of school: desks lined up in rows with the teacher's desk at the front of the room, elementary students lining up to go anywhere, students working individually at their desks rather than in small groups, and heavy reliance on teacher lecture, question/answer-type discussions, and seat work: worksheets, questions at the end of the chapter, and the like. Students have few choices; the teacher makes all major decisions.

The Middle-of-the-Road Approach

Middle-of-the-road schools and classrooms are most prevalent. Here you'll find a mix of methods and some innovative programs. Students will not be so tightly controlled or supervised. In class they will often have small group discussions and projects along with more traditional individual assignments. In general, however, students have more freedom to move around the classrooms than they do in a very traditional school. While the teacher makes all major decisions, students are often invited to participate and make some choices. Each classroom will reflect the basic philosophy of the regular teacher. In a middle-of-the-road school it's possible to find a very conservative old-guard teacher in a room adjacent to one who's very innovative.

Student-Centered Approach

You'll find some schools that still reflect the "free school" practices that were so popular in the late sixties and early seventies. The emphasis in these schools is on student choice and involvement. Thus, students are given more freedom to make decisions about what they will study and how. They often work with other students on projects and spend much less time sitting at their desks doing individual seat work. Many schools are built without walls so students in one class can see (and hear) students in another area. Teachers function more as guides than as sources of knowledge which must be passed on. These schools and classrooms are noisier and more confusing than their traditional couterparts, but that does not mean the students are out of control. They are just learning in different ways, often as much from each other as from the teacher.

Don't assume that you're more apt to have problems with students in a student-centered school that in a more traditional one. It often happens that rigid rules cause students to rebel. I've seen more heated exchanges between teachers and students in tightly-controlled traditionally-run classrooms than in either of the other two types.

The age level of the students seems to make a difference in the philosophical approach a school adopts. Senior high schools are most likely to be very traditional while elementary schools are most likely to be innovative.

ELEMENTARY SCHOOLS

Elementary schools usually include students who are five years old (kindergarten) to those who are ten or eleven (fifth or sixth grade). Most elementary teachers have the same group of students all day long although the students may have other teachers for art, music, and physical education. In very small schools the regular teacher may also teach these subjects as well. The upper grades in many schools are departmentalized, meaning that each teacher has more than one group of students for one subject, such as math. Even in the lower grades in some ungraded schools, students may have different teachers for different blocks of time, but the day is more loosely scheduled than it is when the classes are fully departmentalized at grades five or six and up.

Figure 3

TYPICAL ELEMENTARY TEACHER'S SCHEDULE IN A TRADITIONAL SCHOOL

Before School	No supervision by teachers required
8:55 - 9:05	Take attendance. Collect notes from students. Get hot lunch count. Pledge of Allegiance.
9:05 - 9:15	Sharing (Students bring in items to talk about or just tell what they've done or plan to do.)
9:15 - 10:30	Reading/Language Arts* (Time for each activity varies according to need) Spelling Writing Reading: groups, whole class, small groups needing special help on specific skills (Chapter I aides come into the room to work with individual students who need extra help) Penmanship (not every day; sometimes in P.M.)
10:30 - 10:45	Snacks in classroom (teacher supervises) Students can purchase lunch tickets at cafeteria window, if necessary.
10:45 - 11:00	Recess outside (supervised by each teacher one day a week)
11:00 - 12:00	Math* Individualized, small groups, or whole class (Some students go to a different room if they are working on higher or lower levels than other students in the class)
12:00 - 12:15	Lunch in Cafeteria
12:15 - 12:45	Recess outside (Both lunch and recess supervised by aides)
12:45 - 1:00	Silent reading or teacher or student reads to class
1:00 - 2:45	Science and social studies units Students may spend the whole time on one science or social studies project or time may be divided between the two subjects. Typical units: Explorers (Marco Polo, Columbus, Jacques Cousteau, Sally Ride); Pandas, Puffins, and Penguins; Wind and Weather. (for grade 2 class)
2:45 - 3	Clean up. Stack chairs. Pass out notices and newsletters. Give reminders for next day. Get students ready to leave.
After School	No supervision. Busses pick students up when they leave.

*Several times a week the teacher takes the students to the art, music, or physical education teacher. The regular teacher is free then to do other things. Time missed from the subject scheduled is made up in the afternoon or taken from the undisturbed morning block.

Figure 4

ELEMENTARY TEACHER'S SCHEDULE IN SMALL, UNGRADED SCHOOL

Before School	Supervise students
9:00 - 9:05	Homeroom: Take attendance. Get hot lunch count. Pass out flouride pills.
9:05 - 10:30	READING/LANGUAGE ARTS - Group A* Go over day's schedule which is written on board. Silent Reading (20 minutes)--Every student has an on-going reading book. Spelling (10 minutes) Activities vary during this period: reading groups, dictionary group, individual conferences, short penmanship lessons on some days, individual reading and writing.
10:30 - 10:45	Recess supervised by aides
10:45 - 12:15	READING/LANGUAGE ARTS - Group B* Repeat activities with second group of students.
12:15 - 1:00	Lunch and recess Students eat in classrooms with teachers and then go outside with aides.
1:00 - 1:30	Classroom or (Less often) School Meetings Students participate in informal discussions about feelings, attend grade-based special programs, such as dental health, sex education, etc. Once every three weeks students meet to get information about and to choose upcoming afternoon interdisciplinary elective unit.
1:30 - 2:40	Afternoon Elective Units Three-week units have social studies, science, and arts themes. Specialists in art and music also conduct classes with different groups of students during this time, freeing the regular teacher for other activities.
2:40 - 2:50	Homeroom (with original morning group) Students get notes, notices, and newsletters to take home.
After School	Supervise students until busses leave

*Other teachers teach math during this time block with other groups of students.

There are obvious advantages to having the same group of students all day. It's easier to learn students' names, and the teacher, having control over much of the schedule, can use recess or free time as a means of getting students to complete the assigned work. If the group is a difficult one, however, there's no hope of having a better group to work with later in the day.

Elementary teachers may be responsible for the supervision of students on the playground at recess, lunch, and before and after school until the children are safely inside the building or on the busses. Teachers are expected to teach many subjects, including reading, language arts, math, social studies, science, health, penmanship, and spelling among others. While there may be some flexibility to the daily schedule, many activities must be organized and carried out during the course of the day. Teachers may also have to collect lunch or milk money and take care of other non-teaching chores as well.

Elementary students can be very enthusiastic about learning. Their energy levels can be high and their attention spans, short. The teacher has to help students focus on the task at hand, keep some students from playing too roughly, and settle small squabbles between others--all this while covering the lesson plans, watching the schedule and the clock, and finding ways to occupy students who finish the assignment way ahead of the rest of the class. Because of their relatively short attention spans, students should be involved in a variety of shorter activities during the day.

The teacher may have to assist younger students with buttons, zippers, and shoe laces as well as the more "educational" tasks. Elementary students look up to teachers; love to help out with chores, such as cleaning the chalkboard; or enjoy doing errands, taking notes to the office; but they, too, will test the substitute teacher to see what they can get away with. The students themselves can be a big help in interpreting the teacher's lesson plans since they know the daily routine.

If you substitute in an elementary school which has adopted the new "whole language" approach to teaching reading and writing, you'll find that instead of reading stories in the basal readers, doing worksheets, and meeting in leveled reading groups, students are writing their own books, meeting in small groups with classmates and/or with the teacher to revise them, and "publishing" their final stories in books which are added to the classroom library for others to read. Students in these classrooms will also be choosing other books from the school or classroom libraries to read in class and on their own as well as using reading and writing to learn other subjects, such as social studies, science, and math. "Whole language classrooms" are student-centered rather than teacher-centered in their philosophical approach to education.

MIDDLE SCHOOLS/JUNIOR HIGH SCHOOLS

Middle schools/junior high schools most often include students from ten or eleven to fourteen years of age, fifth or sixth grade through eighth or ninth grades. These schools are usually departmentalized with teachers teaching one or two subjects to several groups of students. A teacher at this level will probably have a homeroom or advisor group for a short time in the morning followed by four or five groups of students from the same grade for their subject (usually reading, language arts, math, science, or social studies). The teacher may also offer an exploratory or elective course at some time during the day. Sometimes classes are ability-grouped, but the trend today is to move away from that practice. Art, music, physical education, home economics, industrial arts, and foreign language teachers have a full schedule teaching their subjects to students in several grades, sometimes at more than one school.

In many middle schools/junior high schools the teachers of the major subjects at each grade level comprise teams (four teachers to about one hundred students) who decide how the instructional time and the students will be divided and plan and teach interdisciplinary units of study. Instead of always studying each subject separately, students will combine activities in language arts, math, science, and social studies to learn about whales or local history in units lasting a few days or weeks which the grade level team of teachers develops.

Covering for a teacher who is part of a team may be easier in some ways because the other team members are available to assist and advise you. If a team meeting is scheduled for a day when you're substituting, you may not be required to attend, but you may learn a great deal by sitting in on the meeting rather than drinking coffee in the teachers' room.

Figure 5

TYPICAL MIDDLE SCHOOL TEACHER'S SCHEDULE

7:45 - 8:00		Teacher Advisor (Homeroom)
8:00 - 8:45	Period 1	Language Arts 6A
8:50 - 9:35	Period 2	Language Arts 6D
9:40 - 10:25	Period 3	Sixth Grade Team Meeting
10:30 - 11:15	Period 4	Language Arts 6C
11:15 - 11:35		Lunch
11:40 - 12:25	Period 5	Prep Period
12:30 - 1:20	Period 6	Language Arts 6B
1:25 - 2:10	Activity	Junior Great Books discussion

Teachers in the middle school or junior high usually have one period per day free for preparation and conferences. This time can be very useful to the substitute if it comes early in the day. Duties at this level might include study hall or lunch room supervision or bus duty before or after school.

Middle school/junior high students are energy personified. They are growing so rapidly and undergoing such physical changes that they struggle to understand who they are. They can be loud or unwilling to talk at all at an adult. They find it difficult to sit quietly for long periods of time so it's a good idea to find ways to let them move around a little. Older students seem far more interested in social activities than they do in school work. Younger students, especially boys, like to rough house with each other.

The teacher must strike the fine balance between friendliness and firmness since these students will challenge authority, most often when they are confronted by an overbearing adult. These students, however, still want to be accepted by adults and like to help out with chores and errands. Their attention spans are longer, and they can get very involved in and enthusiastic about activities in the classroom in which they are interested. Teachers at this level must enjoy pre-teens as people and have large amounts of patience and persistence. A good sense of humor is mandatory!

SENIOR HIGH SCHOOLS

Most senior high schools are completely departmentalized, each teacher usually teaches only one subject area although the content of individual courses may vary. At the high school level some advanced courses, such as calculus, physics, or foreign languages are difficult to cover with substitutes knowledgeable in those areas. For day-to-day substituting school administrators usually expect that the substitute teacher will supervise study sessions rather than conduct regular classes in those subjects. Individuals with expertise in the subject areas would be hired for long-term substituting. Teachers at the senior high level generally teach five classes with a duty (study hall, lunch or hall supervision), homeroom, and one free period for preparation. Vocational classes in various trades--plumbing, auto mechanics and the like--may be offered in high school or at a separate vocational school in the area.

Senior high school students are more mature and independent than those in junior high. The halls are quieter when classes change, and the incidents of rough housing are at a minimum. Depending upon the school, drugs, alcohol, and fighting may be problems, but the teacher is less apt to see these kinds of situations in the classroom than in the bathrooms or smoking area if there is one. Since many high schools have

Figure 6

TYPICAL HIGH SCHOOL TEACHERS' SCHEDULES

		English Teacher	Science Teacher	Math Teacher
7:45 - 7:55	1	Homeroom	Homeroom	Hall Duty
8:00 - 8:50	1	English II General	College Biology	Algebra II
8:50 - 9:45	2	English II General	College Biol. Lab	Algebra II
9:50 - 10:40	3	English II College	General Science	Study Hall
10:45 - 11:35	4	Study Hall	Study Hall	Prep Period
11:35 - 11:55		A Lunch/11:35-12:30 5 Earth Science		General Math
11:55 - 12:50	5	English II Honors/12:30-12:50 B Lunch		B Lunch
12:55 - 1:45	6	Supervise Writing Lab	Prep Period	Algebra I
1:50 - 2:40	7	Prep Period	General Science	Algebra I

recently eliminated smoking areas, some now have teachers assigned to bathroom supervision to prevent smoking in the restrooms. In one school where teachers are scheduled for restroom supervision during only part of the day, the restroom area is a disaster: toilet seats have numerous deep cigarette burns, floors are littered with butts and other trash, and the walls are covered with obscene drawings and messages. If you haven't been in such places recently, you may be shocked at the deplorable conditions you'll find.

Teenagers will challenge authority and can be difficult with a substitute, testing to see how far they can go. The substitute must be firm and self-confident, letting students know who is in charge without fierce confrontations. If asked in front of other students, high school students aren't quick to help the teacher out by doing errands, but they can be counted on for assistance in more subtle ways. Talking to an individual student privately will be more beneficial than asking for a volunteer from the whole class. Students at this age are more apt to be missing from class than younger students. Thus, taking accurate attendance is very important.

WHAT YOU SHOULD KNOW ABOUT SPECIAL EDUCATION

All public schools now have special education classes. These classes are for physically, mentally, or emotionally handicapped students. The small number of severely mentally retarded students usually remains in their own self-contained classroom except for eating lunch in the cafeteria or perhaps attending a regular art class. The most common placement for special ed students, however, is the noncategorical resource room where students from several grades and with a variety of learning problems come for instruction in reading or math or assistance with other school subjects. Students usually attend classes in the resource room for only one or two periods per day. The rest of the day they go to regular classes with the other students.

If you substitute in a regular elementary classroom, you'll probably know who the special ed students are because they will leave your class for part of the day to go to the resource room, a speech therapist, or a physical therapist. Gifted/talented programs in some schools are also pullout programs, i.e. students leave the regular class to go to a special instructor at various times. A deaf or blind student may be assisted throughout the day by his/her own aide.

Special education came into its own and grew rapidly after P.L. 94-142 went into effect in 1977. The law mandated that handicapped students must be placed in the "least restrictive environment," and mainstreamed, that is, placed in regular classes whenever possible. The implementation of this law meant that many students who formerly went to special schools or stayed in classrooms separate from regular students all of the time must now be accommodated in the public schools with other students and taken out of regular classes for special help only when necessary.

Schools must follow a fairly complex and lengthly process to determine appropriate placement for these special needs students. If a teacher feels a student in his/her class may have a learning disability, he/she must fill out a form requesting that the student be considered for special help and documenting both what the problem appears to be and the steps he/she has already taken to address it. A pupil evaluation team (PET) meeting will then be scheduled. The PET usually consists of a regular teacher, a special education teacher, an administrator, the child's parents, and perhaps other teachers and specialists. The team reviews the child's school records, discusses the present situation, and decides whether the student needs further testing. If so, the child is tested by a specialist.

When the test results are available, another team meeting is held. The team reviews the test results and decides on an individualized educational plan (IEP) for the student. The IEP describes what the student's program will be, lists the student's strengths and weaknesses, and identifies both long and short term goals. The parent must sign the IEP. The school cannot take any steps without involving the parent; parents who disagree with a recommended placement can appeal the decision. Each child's IEP must be reviewed in another meeting at least once a year, but meetings are held on many students much more often since a student's program cannot be changed without the approval of the pupil evaluation team and the development of a new or revised IEP.

Special education placement can range from something as simple and inexpensive as the special education teacher giving the regular teacher suggestions and material for working with the student in the regular class or having the student go to the resource room during study halls for special help on regular assignments to something as complicated and expensive as finding treatment for a child in a special residential school which may cost the school district $25,000 or more per student per year. In practice, few students get residential treatment. The largest number of students is served by the noncategorical resource room right in the school.

Substitutes are often needed for the resource room. Classes are smaller than regular classes with perhaps only six to eight students per teacher, but most students require one-to-one instruction. Their learning problems may be due to perceptual difficulties, low intelligence or emotional problems. The resource teacher may have some students on behavior contracts. Students will probably be in the resource room for part of the day, going to regular classes for the remainder. Lesson plans then are different for each child each period. Fortunately there are usually two or more adults working in the resource room--two teachers or one teacher and an aide--so you'll probably find someone to help you sort things out if you come in as a substitute.

Since the routine is so different from a regular classroom and since these students can be difficult to handle, you should visit these classes and talk with the instructors before attempting to substitute for them unless you have training in special education. However, if you can establish rapport with them, these students can be among the most rewarding with whom to work, but it takes a special kind of individual to be a successful special education teacher.

WHERE SHOULD YOU TEACH?

Think about your preferences and abilities. The more subjects and grade levels you are willing to teach, the greater the number of opportunities for employment. With which students will you feel more comfortable? Since high school work is more advanced, you may not feel good about teaching English or math at that level. On the other hand, you may feel more confident about your ability to handle the subject matter with several groups of students than you do about keeping the same thirty noisy elementary youngsters busy for a whole day.

If you think you need more information to make this decision, visit some schools in your area and observe the differences firsthand. After you try substituting at various levels for a while, you may find that you prefer certain age groups, subjects, or even particular schools or classes. You can let the people in charge know your preferences and accept only the assignments you choose. If you find you like high school students but feel uncomfortable because you're rusty on the subject matter, go to the library or arrange to borrow some books from the school to do some review work on your own in those subjects you want to teach. The best teachers are lifelong learners.

Chapter Three

HOW DO YOU GO ABOUT GETTING HIRED?

Y OU'LL HAVE TO do a little research before you begin substitute
teaching in a new area, but in most places actually getting hired
will not be a difficult job.

Take some time to gather copies of all your school records, transcripts, and the like. If you don't have copies of college transcripts, write
to your colleges and have them sent to you.

Although you probably won't need a formal résumé to apply for a job
as a day-to-day substitute teacher, you will need to have the information
that normally appears in a résumé to refer to when you fill out job appli-
cations and go for interviews. Make lists of all of your previous employment experiences and the schools and colleges you've attended along
with the number of credits you've earned in your major and minor subjects and in education courses, if you've taken any.

Probably the most helpful information, however, is a list of all of your
experiences with children. These activities need not be formal employment but any informal or formal activities in which you've worked with
children, both paid and volunteer work. Child care, coaching, tutoring,
church school teaching, and youth group leading are all good preparation for substitute teaching. The more interaction you've had with
young people, the more qualified you are to substitute.

When you've finished gathering all this personal information, you're
ready to take the first step in finding a job.

WHAT TO DO FIRST

Because procedures differ in each state, refer to the chart to see what
office you should contact first in your state. Some states require state

certification so you'll have to file an application with the state department of education before you can formally apply to teach locally. The appendix contains a complete list of the state departments of education.

Figure 7

WHAT OFFICE SHOULD A PROSPECTIVE SUBSTITUTE TEACHER
CONTACT FIRST?

ALABAMA - COUNTY OR CITY SUPERINTENDENT
ALASKA - DISTRICT SUPERINTENDENT OR STATE DEPARTMENT OF EDUCA-
TION (Some districts require certification; others don't.)
ARIZONA - STATE DEPARTMENT OF EDUCATION
ARKANSAS - DISTRICT SUPERINTENDENT
CALIFORNIA - DISTRICT SUPERINTENDENT
COLORADO - DISTRICT SUPERINTENDENT
CONNECTICUT - DISTRICT SUPERINTENDENT
DELAWARE - DISTRICT SUPERINTENDENT
WASHINGTON, D.C. - CERTIFICATION OFFICE, D.C. PUBLIC SCHOOLS
FLORIDA - DISTRICT SUPERINTENDENT
GEORGIA - COUNTY SUPERINTENDENT
HAWAII - DISTRICT SUPERINTENDENT
IDAHO - DISTRICT SUPERINTENDENT
ILLINOIS - COUNTY SUPERINTENDENT
IOWA - STATE DEPARTMENT OF EDUCATION
INDIANA - STATE DEPARTMENT OF EDUCATION
KANSAS - STATE DEPARTMENT OF EDUCATION
KENTUCKY - COUNTY SUPERINTENDENT
LOUISIANA - COUNTY SUPERINTENDENT
MAINE - DISTRICT SUPERINTENDENT
MARYLAND - SCHOOL DISTRICT PERSONNEL OFFICE
MASSACHUSETTS - DISTRICT SUPERINTENDENT OR SCHOOL PRINCIPAL
MICHIGAN - DISTRICT SUPERINTENDENT
MINNESOTA - STATE DEPARTMENT OF EDUCATION
MISSISSIPPI - DISTRICT SUPERINTENDENT
MISSOURI - DISTRICT SUPERINTENDENT
MONTANA - DISTRICT SUPERINTENDENT
NEBRASKA - STATE DEPARTMENT OF EDUCATION
NEVADA - STATE DEPARTMENT OF EDUCATION
NEW HAMPSHIRE - DISTRICT SUPERINTENDENT
NEW JERSEY - COUNTY SUPERINTENDENT
NEW MEXICO - DISTRICT SUPERINTENDENT
NEW YORK - LOCAL SCHOOL DISTRICT PERSONNEL OFFICE
NORTH CAROLINA - COUNTY SUPERINTENDENT
NORTH DAKOTA - STATE DEPARTMENT OF EDUCATION
OHIO - DISTRICT SUPERINTENDENT
OKLAHOMA - DISTRICT SUPERINTENDENT
OREGON - TEACHER STANDARDS AND PRACTICES COMMISSION, STATE
DEPT. OF EDUCATION
PENNSYLVANIA - STATE DEPARTMENT OF EDUCATION

Figure 7(Continued)

RHODE ISLAND - STATE DEPARTMENT OF EDUCATION
SOUTH CAROLINA - DISTRICT SUPERINTENDENT
SOUTH DAKOTA - DISTRICT SUPERINTENDENT
TENNESSEE - COUNTY SUPERINTENDENT
TEXAS - DISTRICT SUPERINTENDENT
UTAH - DISTRICT SUPERINTENDENT
VERMONT - SCHOOL PRINCIPAL
VIRGINIA - STATE DEPARTMENT OF EDUCATION
WASHINGTON - STATE DEPARTMENT OF EDUCATION
WEST VIRGINIA - COUNTY SUPERINTENDENT
WISCONSIN - STATE DEPARTMENT OF EDUCATION
WYOMING - DISTRICT SUPERINTENDENT

Even if you're located in a state which requires state certification, however, you may find it more convenient to contact the office of the local superintendent of schools first because many times someone there can explain the certification requirements and furnish you with copies of any state forms needed.

If your state does not require state certification, your first call will be to the local (county or school district) superintendent's office. The local superintendent in some states is responsible for certification of substitute teachers. In Maine, for example, the superintendent's office determines who is qualified and merely sends a list of the individuals who will substitute in local schools to the state department of education. In such cases the process for you is very simple because all you have to do is file an application in each district in which you'd like to substitute.

WHERE YOU WILL SUBSTITUTE

You'll need to make some decisions about where you are willing to substitute and figure out how many school districts comprise that geographical area.

What schools are nearby? Take a map of your area and decide how far you can reasonably travel to substitute either by car or public transportation. Draw a circle around this area on the map. List the different communities which fall within this circle and find out how they are organized into school districts.

In Florida, for example, the schools are organized by counties. Your task in this case will be much easier because if the circle you've drawn falls within one county, one trip to the office of the superintendent of schools will tell you all you need to know about substituting in any area school. In most other places schools are organized separately by communities or in school districts where several smaller towns join to form one district.

The phone book will help you locate the superintendents you need to contact. The phone book also lists all the schools in a district as well so you can see how many elementary, secondary, or vocational schools come under a district's jurisdiction and their locations. Take some time to compare these listings with the circle you have drawn on the map.

CONTACTING LOCAL SUPERINTENDENTS

Call the district offices of the communities in which you think you'd like to sub. Ask if you need an appointment to talk with someone or if it is okay for you to just drop in.

Your visit to the office of the superintendent of schools should provide you with all the information you need to substitute in the district's schools. You don't have to talk with the superintendent personally. A secretary can tell you what you need to know and can schedule an appointment with the personnel office if necessary. In many smaller communities you may only have to complete an application to be put on the substitute list.

Be sure to bring the following with you: an updated or informal copy of your résumé, transcripts of any college courses you have taken, and, if you have any, copies of your teacher certification--even if expired. In some states the requirements for substituting include any teacher certificate whether expired or from another state. Don't forget to bring a notebook!

Questions To Ask

What are the requirements for substituting in local schools?

You can find out whether or not you qualify and what you need to do to begin substituting. For example, TB tests are required for all school personnel in some places.

How does one apply to substitute?

The application is usually furnished by the central office so the secretary can give you the necessary application and employment forms and perhaps schedule appointments for interviews if they are needed. If you apply directly to the state for certification, the secretary probably has this form as well or can tell you how to get one. You may find that you can take care of all the necessary paperwork and be put on the district's substitute list by the end of your visit.

How often are substitutes needed?

The secretary can give you a general idea of how often substitutes are needed and how many people are available to substitute. Don't worry if the pool seems too large. Many people put their names on the list, find other employment, and then forget to remove their names. You can register to substitute at any time during the year.

Since most districts advertise and develop their lists in the fall, the number of substitutes still available in the spring is greatly diminished. If you add your name in the spring, you'll probably be called right away. Because people change their minds or their plans so frequently, the substitute list at all times is much longer than the actual number of people who are available to substitute on a regular basis.

Who hires the substitutes?

The answer to this question is very important because it will tell you what you need to do to get called after you are on the list. Perhaps the principals or department heads do the calling or it may be a central office or school secretary or even the teachers themselves. You need to make sure that whoever does the calling knows who you are so that you are not just a name on a list.

Depending upon the answer to this question, make plans to schedule appointments with principals, department heads, or whomever. All you have to do is meet briefly with them to let them know you are available to substitute and to pick up some pointers to help you out when you do substitute in these schools. Once you have done some substituting and shown that you are capable, teachers will request that you be called to replace them.

Are there any substitute orientation or training programs?

If the district has an orientation or training program for substitutes, you'll want to attend. Not only will you meet people who count in getting hired, but you will also get much useful background to make your substituting easier.

What opportunities exist for school volunteers?

Why should you volunteer your services when you want to get paid? Simply because volunteering is another way to meet the people who do the hiring and the best means of finding out how the schools operate as well as getting to know the students and teachers. Ask the secretary which schools use volunteers and whom you should contact regarding volunteering.

If you are looking for a fulltime teaching job, volunteering can lead to substituting which can lead to employment as a regular teacher. The contacts you will make and the experiences you gain in the process will be beneficial to you both personally and professionally. One young mother returning to the work force with no previous paid experience landed a newly created career guidance position because of the people she knew and the personal reputation she had established as a coordinator for the volunteer program in her community's schools.

Through working as a substitute teacher, you may find employment on a regular basis as a teacher aide or assitant teacher. Duties for these positions are varied and may range from working directly with students by giving individual help in reading or math to supervising study halls or lunch rooms and providing clerical assistance to teachers. These positions, although not high-paying ones, usually require only six hours per day or less, and school vacations are still free for your other pursuits. Some college may be required, but you do not have to be a college graduate or trained teacher to fill them.

What copies of district and school publications are available?

While your main purpose in visiting the superintendent's office is completing necessary forms and getting a list of people along with their phone numbers to contact about getting into the schools, you may be able to get more information about the schools in the system as well. Ask if there are any brochures, handbooks, newsletters, student publications, or pamphlets with information for substitute teachers available. The school district's philosophy and a complete listing of pertinent information about all of the schools in a district may appear in a copy of the district's teacher handbook.

Ask for copies of materials to take home to read more carefully. If none is available for you to keep, take a few minutes to skim the materials in the office and jot down a few notes. You can learn a great deal from reading any school publications which are available.

How much are substitutes paid? When and how are pay checks issued?

Ask about the rate of pay and whether or not it's possible to earn more than minimum. The more qualified people and those hired on a long-term basis will probably earn more than the minimum, but some districts raise the daily rate of pay when a person teaches for more that ten days a year even when those days are not consecutive. Although few districts offer benefits to substitutes, ask if there are any. In some states you can earn credit towards retirement by substituting a certain number of days per year.

Find out how long it takes for a substitute to be paid. The pay period will probably be determined by the system's payroll schedule. If teachers are paid only every two weeks, then a substitute may have to wait two weeks or a month for the first pay check to be issued. Ask if the checks are mailed or must be picked up somewhere. The office secretary can explain all of these procedures to you or can refer you to someone else who will know.

When you leave the superintendent's office, you should be knowledgeable enough to take the next steps: calling and visiting individual schools, applying to the state, or planning what you need to do before the first day of substitute teaching.

Repeat the procedure described here for each district in which you think you'd like to work. Since the need for substitutes is uneven, you'll have a greater chance for continuous employment if you're on the substitute lists of several neighboring school districts. After you've gained some experience, you'll find that you prefer a certain school or district because you seem to fit in better, the students are more well behaved, the staff is friendlier, or the location is closer to your home, Then you may want to limit your scope, but don't do that now when you are just beginning.

Even if you discover that you must apply to the state for a substitute certificate before you can begin working, you don't have to put everything on hold. Use the time in the interim to learn more about the schools by visiting them or serving as a volunteer.

No special piece of paper is required for volunteer work. You might approach the teachers in a school where you think you'd like to sub and offer to assist them by tutoring students who need remedial help or by correcting papers. You'll get to know the teachers and the students while you're getting valuable information about teaching by observing the normal classroom routines.

Two parents in one middle school got in-depth experience and helped the school out by working with language arts teachers and students to produce a student newspaper for the school. They saw a need in the school no one else was addressing and won the principal's support for the project as well as her undying gratitude. Later they both worked regularly and very successfully as substitute teachers in the school.

Scheduling a brief conference with the principal, department heads, or team leaders is a good way to find out what the school's needs for volunteers and substitute teachers are. It's also a good way to make yourself known and become more knowledgeable about the school and its expectations and deficiencies. While you won't earn any money as a volunteer, you'll feel good about yourself, and you'll have another credit to add to your résumé.

Chapter Four

PLANNING FOR THE FIRST DAY

GETTING TO KNOW THE SCHOOL BEFORE YOU GO

THE MORE you know about individual schools before you substitute, the more confident you will be on your first day. Confidence in doing the job is a prerequisite for controlling students and preventing discipline problems. If you aren't able to do any observing or volunteering in a school, become as familiar as you can with the school, its curriculum, policies, and schedule by reading newsletters and guides you picked up at the superintendent's office or at the school and any notes you may have taken.

Useful written materials you can request at the school's office include curriculum guides, school schedule, student and teacher handbooks, school newspapers, yearbooks, map of the school, course of study handbooks, and substitute handbook, if there is one. Becoming familiar with the physical layout of the building by studying the map or by attending an open house is also a good idea.

Talk to people who work at the school. Cafeteria workers and custodians as well as secretaries and teachers can provide you with a great deal of information. Parents of children who attend the school are yet another resource. Consider the source of your information though and realize that the viewpoint you're getting may be biased. The mother of a boy who hasn't done well and always seems to get into trouble at school may have very negative feelings about the way the school is run. Her feelings will probably not be shared by most other parents.

All of this is easier, of course, if you're planning to sub at only one school. If you'll be working at several schools, you'll have to find out about each school when you go, but the suggestions above will still be useful. If you glance at the most recent issue of the student newspaper while you're having coffee in the teachers' room before school, mentioning something you read to your first group of students will get you off to a good start. Not only will you show them that you're interested in them, you'll also create the illusion that you know what's going on in the school. Because the students will get the impression that you're familiar with the school, they'll be less likely to try to manipulate you into letting them do things they are not normally allowed to do. Students often get the upper hand with substitute teachers because they know that they know more about the school than the sub does. You don't actually have to know more than the students to put yourself in a good position. Just make them think that you do!

KEEPING A JOURNAL OR NOTEBOOK

If you've had the opportunity to keep a journal at some time in the past, then you already know how useful such writing can be. Get a notebook especially for jotting down information about each school and writing down your impressions and experiences every time you substitute.

Set aside part of the notebook for general information about schools. Make a section for each school and record here useful information you've already gathered: address, phone, principal's name, daily schedule, etc. Whenever you sub in that school, add other general information which will be useful to remember. Before you go to that school, you can refresh your memory about particular details by reading through your notes.

Establish another section for notes on activities you try and how they go. If you're going to sub at several levels, you may wish to make separate categories for elementary, middle school, and high school. If you develop your own materials for some activities, make a note here to remind you what you have and where it's located so you can easily find and use a successful activity another time.

Probably the most useful part of your notebook will be the daily journal section. Every time you substitute, sit down for ten minutes or so at the end of the day and write freely about what you did, what the students did, and what you learned or would like to know. If you faced a difficult situation and weren't sure what you should have done, you may be surprised to discover that you'll find the answer as you write about it.

Even though you won't be able to go back and handle that student in a different way, you'll remember what you found out this time when a similar situation occurs in the future.

Your journal is also a good place to record what you don't know and would like to. You won't have much time during the day to seek out answers to your questions, but if you jot them down, you can ask another teacher for advice or do further reading on your own to find answers later. You'll find that your journal will not only help you become a better substitute teacher, but it will also be fun to go back and read months or years later. When you collect enough of your experiences in the journal, you may even decide you want to write a book!

WHAT TO WEAR

Although few schools enforce dress policies these days the way they used to, you will make a better impression on the adults and appear more businesslike to students if your attire is neat and conservative.

For women a dress, suit, or skirt and blouse with a blazer or cardigan sweater are good. Men should wear a suit or sport jacket and slacks with shirt and tie or turtleneck. Stay away from jeans and clothing that is tight-fitting or loose and baggy. Women should avoid excessive makeup, jangling jewelry, and heavy perfume. Both men and women should be clean, neat, and well-groomed.

Students probably won't say much about how you look, but they will notice. Too casual or informal an appearance will cause students to act too casually when you're trying to teach. Unusual clothing or personal habits will cause problems for a new person in the school because students are quick to ridicule or make fun of anyone who appears even a little out of the ordinary. One student teacher had a very difficult time establishing himself with his high school students because he was carrying a man's purse in the European style the first day he came to school. The students were sure he was a "fag." Although they finally were willing to overlook this idiosyncracy in his case, it took him several weeks to get them to look "beyond his purse." As a day-to-day substitute teacher, you won't have that much time with the same group of students so first impressions are even more important.

You may notice when you arrive at the school that some regular teachers are dressed very casually. Some may not realize that their dress is a handicap. When I was a principal, one parent, after a conference with all of her son's teachers, asked me why the custodian had been included in the conference. At first I was confused, but further conversation revealed that she was referring to her son's math teacher! Because he wore loosely-fitting gray work pants with a matching gray work shirt, he certainly did look more like a custodian that a teacher.

This math teacher, like most other regular teachers, had already established his reputation with students and so he could get away with poorly chosen clothing. You, however, don't need an additional hurdle to jump the first day. Besides, you won't risk offending anyone by your appearance if you're dressed neatly and conservatively.

WHAT TO TAKE

Anytime you substitute, you should be prepared for any contingency.

The first day you substitute at a new school, you'll find it helpful if you bring your own bag lunch. After you're there and see how the schedule works and what the cafeteria lunches are like, you may prefer to skip the bag lunch next time. Although most teachers today are guaranteed a duty-free lunch period, you may find that circumstances make it impossible or undesirable for you to eat at the scheduled time. If you bring your lunch, you can eat later or earlier instead of skipping the meal altogether.

You should also bring a substitute survival kit. You can't count on finding carefully written lesson plans when you sub. Most teachers will leave plans, but others leave nothing! I once substituted for a week for a teacher who left nothing: no plans, books, or seating charts. After talking to students and other teachers and searching around in the classroom debris, I finally figured out what social studies units the classes were supposed be doing and developed my own plans. When I was unavailable to continue subbing the second week, the principal asked ME to leave plans for the new substitute!

Read through the activities and suggestions in Part II of this book and choose several that you could use with the grade levels and subject areas you're likely to teach. Make up class sets of the materials you'll need. Choose some stories you can read aloud to younger students and puzzles or thinking games you can do with older students.

Your survival kit should include both activities which will fill a whole period in case a film is scheduled and doesn't arrive and those which can be used as fillers when students finish an assignment early and there are still ten minutes left until the bell. You invite problems when you give most students unstructured time to use as they wish. "You may talk quietly until the bell rings" may sound like a logical thing to say, but you'll often find that the noise level will increase to undesirable levels very quickly, students will get out of their seats and wander about the room or out in the hall, and some boys will begin roughhousing with each other or teasing the girls. Giving students time to work on their homework often produces similar results. If students have study hall next period, they may figure they'll do it then. Many students don't want to do homework at school because they would rather spend the time socializing with their friends, something they can't do at home.

Writing assignments that can take up a whole period or just a few minutes can be very useful for students in any grade in any subject. In the next chapter you'll find some ways to use writing in any class. Jot down the ideas that you think you'd like to use and add them to your survival kit.

What's most important to take along when you substitute, however, are some thoughtfully planned ways of avoiding problems with students and strategies for handling the situations you couldn't prevent or anticipate. Reading and thinking about potential problems before you go is probably the best way to reduce the number you'll face.

PLANNING AHEAD TO MINIMIZE PROBLEMS

When you actually look at the means regular teachers and even principals have to get students to behave, you'll see that penalties and punishment are very limited. Beyond taking away privileges, keeping students in at recess or after school, assigning them to an in-school suspension room, or sending them home on an out-of-school suspension, there isn't much either a teacher or principal can do. Students who don't like school will be very happy to be sent home. You may be surprised to learn that the force of your own personality, not punishments and penalties, is the most effective tool you have for getting students to do what's expected. Of course, you will find that consequences for inappropriate behavior are useful, but don't depend on them to prevent problems. Consequences come only AFTER a student has already misbehaved. The way to make teaching more enjoyable for you and your students is to find ways to avoid having to reach the point where consequences and penalties are needed.

Haim Ginott sees discipline as a "series of little victories." These little victories begin with helping students develop better self-concepts or self-images. It's very important to remember that people who feel good about themselves always do better in school and in life than those who feel inferior, worthless, and lonely. Children are no different. You need to interact with them in ways that make them feel more successful and worthwhile rather than less so.

When you have to deal with students who misbehave, try to do so in a way that doesn't make students feel put down or ridiculed. Leave them a way to save face. Anger, unless used rarely and then only feigned for an effect, is ineffective as are sarcasm and insults. I spent almost two full years as a middle school principal before any student saw me angry or heard me shout. Near the end of the second year I was trying to talk to a sixth grade boy who just wouldn't listen. Finally, although I wasn't angry, I pretended to be and yelled at him. Because he had never heard me raise my voice before, he stopped talking mid-sentence. I was able to finish our discussion in a normal voice because he was finally listening instead of yapping. This technique worked only because my behavior came as a surprise to him. If anger and shouting were my normal style, he would have paid no attention. How many children never hear their mother's constant nagging or pay attention to her threats? Real anger is a signal to students that you have lost control. If you're not in control, who is? The students, and, believe me, they not only will know it, they'll also take advantage of you.

Physical means to get students to do anything should NEVER be used. In many states it's illegal to touch students except to keep them from physically hurting themselves or others. You set yourself up for a great deal of difficulty, possibly even a lawsuit, if you lay a hand on a student. Besides, if you focus on developing positive relationships with students rather than on penalties and punishments, you'll rarely find yourself in situations where you feel like strangling or spanking some kid.

Consider how you like people to treat you and treat students the same way. Be kind, polite, helpful, and friendly. Say "please" and "thank you" even when students don't. Avoid confrontations, demands, and putdowns. Some students, especially teenagers, instinctively rebel when given a command. Make requests instead. Use positive "I" rather than negative "you" statements: Not "Stay in your seat," but "I'd like you to stay in your seats;" not "Be quiet," but "I'd like everyone to listen." If you're not used to dealing with children (even your own) in this manner, practice. You'll be amazed at the results you can get just by changing slightly the wording you use.

Above all, don't take students' misbehavior personally. Remember their days can get off to a bad start just as yours can. Their actions in class may be the result of something that happened at home or on the way to school. If you deal with a situation firmly but matter-of-factly, students are more apt to respond positively. If you act emotionally rather than logically, students will, too. If you get angry, they will, too. Students tend to mirror the behavior of the teacher.

Finally, talking with students privately is always much better if you can manage it than dealing with them in front of the whole class. Students are on stage if other students are watching and will usually behave differently when they are alone with you. The mystery you create by talking to a student who has misbehaved at your desk or in the hall will help you keep the whole class in line. Since the other students don't know what you said or did, they'll imagine worse consequences than you probably delivered and will want to avoid meeting the same fate.

DEVELOPING YOUR OWN CLASSROOM MANAGEMENT PLAN

Before you go into the classroom, you must have established your expectations for students and decided the consequences for those who do not meet them. Everything happens so fast in a classroom and there are so many things you have to think about at once, you won't have a quick solution for a situation unless you've planned what you might do in advance. You'll feel more confident when you know what you're going to do, and your confidence will show. Students are much less likely to challenge someone who appears to be sure of himself or herself and will go for the jugular if a substitute appears unsure or wishy-washy. Note the use of the word "appears." Even if you don't feel confident, act as though you are and soon you will be.

The fewer rules you have the better. No more than four or five are best, but don't begin by writing rules down. Instead list all of the behaviors you can think of that you don't want to occur in your class: talking while you're talking, getting up and walking around the room, poking another student, sleeping in class, looking out the window, fighting, etc.

Divide your list into two categories: those that disturb others and those which interfere only with the learning of a single individual. Be prepared to deal immediately and effectively with students whose behavior is keeping others from learning, but plan to ignore--or at least consider a lower priority--the student who sits quietly daydreaming while the other students are writing their stories.

Consequences for not meeting your expectations need to be thought out in advance and communicated clearly to students. The consequences should be logical in terms of the misbehavior which prompts their use, and they need to be effective in terms of letting students know that such misbehavior will not be tolerated.

The consequences also have to fit some kind of hierarchical order. You obviously can't send a student who's whispering to the student beside him to the principal or vice-principal. What would you do then when you need more severe consequences, when two students are fighting, for example?

Sending students to the office is generally not an effective technique since the message you give to students is that you aren't in control. The principal, not you, has power. You may feel that you don't have any power, but you must act as though you do. Being a good disciplinarian is as simple and as complex as having a few necessary rules with logical consequences if they are broken, and, after making sure that students understand both, following through with the stated consequences whenever a rule is broken.

YOU MUST BE CONSISTENT! You can't ignore one student's misbehavior and then nail another student later for doing the same thing. You can't tell a student that she'll lose her recess and then let her go outside with everyone else. At least you can't do these things and expect the students to behave. It's very important that **you treat everyone the same way and that you do what you say you will do.** Otherwise students will resent the fact that you pick on some kids and let others get away with murder and they won't believe what you say when you most need them to do so.

If you are consistent, clear, and fair in your approach to classroom discipline and you project an air of confidence, students will never realize that you feel powerless. Most of the power anyone needs comes from inside rather than outside and is communicated to others by one's attitude and behavior.

Students want to know what adults expect of them. They also want to know what will happen if they cross the line. They want to be treated fairly and consistently. You can be sure in almost every class there will be at least one student who will test you to see if you mean what you say. Some students who misbehave actually calculate their misbehavior. They don't want to get into a lot of trouble, but they don't mind getting hassled or punished by the teacher for little things in order to see how he or she will react. Such a student is apt to be the first one to give you a hard time by refusing to go to his seat or to stop talking when you ask. Deal with that first case well, and you'll prevent other cases from even occurring.

After you outline rules and their consequences, follow through the first time a rule is violated. Do that every time a rule is tested. Do what you said you would do. Say as little as possible; the fewer words you use, the better. Gestures, body language, and eye contact can be very effective. Don't yell, lecture, or insult students. You will soon establish yourself with students as a person who means what he or she says, and they will, for the most part, stop testing you. Once you pass muster with a group of students, you won't have to prove yourself all over again another time. A brief reminder of your expectations will probably be enough. If you substitute frequently in the same school, you'll find that students may already know about you from talking with their friends. You can go in and work with a new group of students without the usual first-day pressures because students have already found out what you expect by word of mouth.

Minor Misbehavior

Look at the original list of misbehavior you developed. Consider first the actions which interfere only with the learning of an individual student. You don't need any consequences for these situations.

As a substitute who only has the class for only one or two days, you do not have much influence on a given student's success or failure in that course or in school. If a student is not paying attention but is not disturbing anyone else, there is really no need for you to do anything. If the rest of the class is working and you can privately talk to such a student and perhaps encourage him or her to work, go ahead. It doesn't, however, make any sense to invite a confrontation and risk escalating a situation which affects only one student into one which disturbs the whole class and leaves you frustrated and angry. Better to let the student sit there quietly doing nothing and let the regular teacher know about it in your end-of-the-day note.

Gum chewing is an example of a behavior at the next level up. If a student chews gum discretely, doesn't snap it or blow bubbles, and doesn't stick it on chairs or desks, ignore it. Of course, if it's against the school rules, you should do something, but you don't need consequences for gum chewing. You don't want to end up in a big hassle with a student over something as trivial as a piece of gum. Simply say to the student in a pleasant, matter-of-fact way , "Please throw your gum in the wastebasket." After the student discards the gum, say "thank you."

A similar technique is all you need for students wearing hats in school, playing with wads of paper, and fooling around with "toys" in class. "Please take your hat off." "Please throw the paper in the basket." "Please give me the golf ball. I'll keep it safe for you until the end of the period." In the latter case, don't grab the item. Simply ask the student to hand it to you, put your hand out, and wait. If the student begins to argue, say nothing at first. Just hold your hand there. Then prompt, if necessary with "Please" or repeat your initial request. It's highly unlikely that a student will make a big deal out of such a minor matter when you use this approach. After all, HE knows that he shouldn't have the golf ball in class in the first place.

Misbehavior that does disturb the class needs more attention, but the methods you use should still be low key and matter of fact. You probably have such actions as talking while the teacher's talking, drumming on the desk, and the like on your list. Make a separate list of these behaviors. You don't need consequences for a first offense. First try eye contact and gestures to get the student to do what's expected. If these methods don't work, try a simple request: "Please listen while I'm talking." "Please stop tapping on your desk." If the student continues, you'll have to take more drastic steps. Always begin, however, with the least obtrusive means of correcting the students' minor misbehavior. Save those measures which call more attention to the problem until you have to use them because your first effort didn't work or the problem which occurs is a more serious one when it begins.

Serious Problems Which Violate School Rules

We'll come back to handling the student who continues to misbehave in minor ways, but first consider those situations where the problem is so serious you shouldn't try to deal with it yourself. If two students begin fighting in your classroom, a student appears to be drunk or high on drugs, or a student loses his temper, begins swearing and screaming, you should NOT attempt to deal with them. If you can, send the student(s) to the principal or the vice-principal on their own and ask another student to take a note from you explaining the situation. If the situation is such that the students should or cannot be sent on their own, use the intercom or send a student to summon someone to your room. Call on the teacher in the next classroom if you need help or advice.

You have now listed the very minor problems which you can ignore, minor problems which you should first handle at as low as level as possible, and the most serious ones which you shouldn't attempt to deal with at all. What you have left are several mid-level problems plus what to do with the student who doesn't respond to your initial attempts to deal with a minor problem. The next section will explain what you can do about those cases.

SAMPLE CLASSROOM RULES

RESPECT THE RIGHTS AND PROPERTY OF OTHERS.
LISTEN WHEN SOMEONE TALKS.
RAISE YOUR HAND IF YOU NEED HELP OR HAVE A QUESTION.
BE POLITE AND HELPFUL.

Repeated Misbehavior and More Serious Classroom Problems

If a student continues to misbehave or if a student does something which clearly needs more that an admonishment from you, perhaps yelling across the room to another student in language that's inappropriate for the classroom, resist the urge to get the students out of your hair by sending them to the principal's office.

Instead talk to the student privately. Give the other students something to do: write a summary of the class discussion so far, brainstorm questions they have about the topic under study, read the next section in their text, or do the next problem or question. Take the offender out in the hall or to the back of the room--anywhere where you can talk without other students overhearing the conversation.

The purpose of this brief conference is to get the student to agree to cooperate. Don't make matters worse by attacking the student verbally or delivering a lecture. Simply state that the behavior the student displayed was unacceptable. Ask him/her if there's something you should know that would help explain why it occurred. The possibility exists that what the student was doing was really caused by another student with whom you may also have to chat. If the student doesn't describe any mitigating circumstances, then ask what he/she is going to do about it. Accept any reasonable response the student gives you, but add, "I hope that I won't have to speak to you again about this matter because if I do, I will have to take further action." Of course, you state exactly what the "further action" will be. Then ask the student if he/she understands and to repeat back to you what 1) he/she plans to do when he/she returns to the classroom and 2) what will happen if there are further problems. Thank him/her and send him/her back to class. Pick up with the lesson where you left off.

You have several options for "further action." The next step might be placing the student in a "time out" area in the classroom. Any corner, behind a filing cabinet or bookcase, where the student is separated from other students will do. Place the desk facing the wall so that the student can't see what is going on and make sure students in the class can't see the offender. If necessary, you can place the student outside in the hall, but that may not be a solution if the hall provides any entertainment, such as students walking by or other classes to watch. Students who don't like school may find the hall more interesting than the classroom. You'll also have to remember to check on the student to make sure he/she doesn't wander off.

When you place a student in "time out," he/she should understand that he/she is to remain there, working on an assignment, until he/she can make a commitment to return to the class and behave appropriately and that you will leave a note explaining to the regular teacher what has happened.

Other possibilities for "further action" include keeping a student in at recess, part of lunch, or after school. Since these actions will involve giving up your free time, try to avoid using them, but know that they exist if you have no alternative.

If after a conference, the student continues to misbehave, follow through as you said you would. Tell the student what you are doing and why. Explain that if this action doesn't solve the problem, you will be forced to send him/her to the office. Say, "I really don't want to cause you any further hassles, but I don't want any either. When you're ready to return to the class and behave as you should, let me know, but realize if there is a further problem, you'll have to explain to the principal. I hope we don't reach that point. It won't do either of us any good." Because you are firm, but friendly and fair as you talk to the student, you're very likely to have no further problems.

There is another intermediate step you can take before sending the student to the office, but you should get the principal's permission before using it: taking the student to the nearest phone to call his/her parent (at work, if necessary) to explain why he/she cannot behave appropriately in class. You listen while he/she talks and then take the phone to fill in missing details. Apologize for bothering the parent and thank him/her for helping you out. This technique can be incredibly effective even if you only use it once. Word about the incident will spread throughout the school. Most other students will never risk getting into a situation where you'll make them call their parents! Such phone calls, however, are not effective with older high school students.

This conference method with increasingly more severe consequences works well because what you are doing each time is giving the student a choice: he/she can behave and nothing happens, but if he/she chooses to misbehave, he/she has CHOSEN to be placed in "time out" or to miss half of recess. You haven't done anything to the student. He/she has done it to himself/herself.

By not getting angry and harshly punishing the student, you increase the likelihood that you'll have no further difficulties with the student. Students who are used to being in trouble with the teacher and have spent lots of time getting chewed out and punished may be surprised at first to have an adult treat him firmly but with respect. By inviting the student to explain, you show the student that you do care about his opinions and feelings. It will be difficult for him to be hostile and difficult when you are treating him as a person instead of a bad kid you'd like to get rid of. You can further these good feelings if you also remember to thank him for his cooperation at the end of the day. There would be fewer troublemakers in schools if students were given more responsibility for their own behavior and encouragement and praise when they did make good choices.

Chapter Five

SURVIVING ON THE JOB

FIRST THINGS FIRST

WHEN YOU GO to a school to substitute, try to get there a few minutes early so you'll have time to find your way around--your classroom(s) for the day, the teachers' room, and, of course, the bathroom--read the information left by the teacher, and locate any necessary materials or equipment.

Stop first at the main office to check in, get keys, schedule, daily bulletin, and other notices, Ask if there are any special events scheduled today, such as an assembly. Take a minute to read through your schedule and make sure you understand it. The secretary is a good person to answer questions on any subject related to the school.

When you walk into your classroom, take a deep breath and remember the FIRST thing you have to do is establish order in the class. You won't be able to take attendance or teach anything until students are in their seats, quiet and ready to listen. In order to get the students in line, however, you have to appear confident and in charge. Tell yourself that you are older and more experienced than these students, you planned how you are going to approach the job, and, because you're prepared, you will succeed. Even if you aren't totally sure that's true at this point, pretend that it is. First you'll fool the students, then you'll fool yourself, and then at the end of the day you'll have done such a good job of acting the part, you'll find that you're not acting any more.

Go over the schedule carefully and read the information the teacher left. Find first the things you'll need for homeroom: seating chart, attendance forms, and the like. If the morning announcements aren't read over the P.A., get the printed bulletin ready to read and post.

Next check the schedule, lesson plans, and materials for the rest of the day. Make sure supplementary books and handouts are available. Arrange everything in order according to when the classes meet.

If you get to school early enough, you'll still have time for a cup of coffee in the teachers' room. Get use to people asking, "Who are you today?" Substitute teachers are like chameleons; their identity changes every day. Don't be afraid to ask other teachers for suggestions and advice. The more you know, the better off you'll be.

Get back to the classroom before the students come in. Write your name on the board and any directions students will need when they first come in. Until you're sure how difficult to manage your classes will be, it's not a good idea to write too much on the board during class. You have to turn your back to them, and trouble can occur until you develop those "teacher eyes" in the back of your head.

Station yourself by the door and greet the students as they enter the room. Meeting students at the door is not only a good practice for the first class but also for all others throughout the day. You show that you're interested in the students, that you're prepared and organized, and that you're in charge.

If you spot two students involved in a little horesplay in the hall before classes begin, seize the opportunity to show students you are serious about your work. Calmly but firmly direct them to stop. Call on another teacher or an administrator for assistance if they ignore your request. Most students will comply with a simple, direct request which is delivered in a firm but friendly tone. The fact that you are concerned about student behavior even in the halls lets students know that you will definitely expect them to work and behave in the classroom.

At the beginning of each class, including homeroom, make sure all students are in their seats and paying attention before you begin speaking. Say, "I'd like you to listen please," and wait until you have silence. If the teacher's note doesn't say anything about morning exercises (flag salute, etc.), check with a reliable student, i.e. the quiet one who already has his or her book open ready to go. Don't ever try to talk above the students' talking. If you stand in front of the class LOOKING DIRECTLY at the students and wait, they'll usually quiet down. In fact, those who don't will probably get reminders from their classmates.

Remembering to keep your manner friendly as well as purposeful, introduce yourself and tell students a little about yourself. Unless you have the homeroom students for the first class period as well, you can skip discussing your expectations. With all other classes, however, spend a minute or two explaining your expectations and the simple rules you developed. Point out that sports, families, and governments all have rules and the reasons why they are needed. Ask students if any of your ground rules is unreasonable or if they have any questions about them. Tell them that you expect to have a good day and you'd like for them to have one, too. You understand that it's difficult for them when a stranger comes in for their regular teacher. You hope they'll understand that you won't handle things exactly the way their regular teacher does, but if you make any big mistakes, you'd appreciate their letting you know.

If there are still a few minutes before the bell rings and all the homeroom tasks are done, there's no harm in letting students talk quietly until they leave. They should, however, remain in their seats. If these same students will be with you for first period, and in all other class periods, it's not a good idea to let students have even this small amount of freedom. Some classes can handle the freedom; others can't. You won't know which is which the first day, so keep them busy with a puzzle or writing assignment. See Part II of the book for ideas. Busy students are much less likely to get into trouble.

After opening the first class in the manner described above, get right down to the business at hand. Ask for students' assistance, if necessary, in taking attendance, finding the right forms, and completing routine tasks. If you are substituting for a well-organized teacher, you will find everything spelled out very clearly in the instructions to the substitute. Everything you need from AV materials and equipment to hall passes will be readily available. In other situations you may have to play detective to locate what you need and plan much of the day yourself.

Students may bombard you with requests to go somewhere else: the office, their locker, the library, the bathroom. Discourage all but the most urgent-sounding request, and don't let anyone leave to go anywhere until everyone is seated and quiet and you've finished taking attendance. Have students sign their names on a sheet along with their intended destinations. Then later at your leisure or convenience, allow them to go, one at a time, if the trips are really necessary.

If you begin with an activity students must work on quietly at their desks, you'll be free to handle all the student requests with much less confusion. If the teacher hasn't left such an assignment as part of the lesson plan, use an activity from Chapter Six or Part II of this book. Write the directions on the board so students can begin working as soon as they come into the room.

Once the class has begun, remember your plan. If a student misbehaves, deal with the inappropriate behavior in the manner you've planned. Expect that students will behave positively; most will. You may encounter more difficulty if you substitute for a teacher who has poor classroom control, but I've seen many substitutes handle classes more effectively than the regular teachers do. The students may behave badly in that class one period a day, but you can be sure all their teachers don't allow them to do whatever they wish. Students will get away with exactly as much as a given teacher allows. If you refuse to tolerate unacceptable behavior when you're in charge, most students will accommodate their actions to your expectations.

WHERE TO GET ADVICE AND ASSISTANCE IN THE SCHOOL

Depending upon the size of the school, you can get information and assistance from a variety of people. In a small school the principal will be available to help with just about anything. In a larger school you may never see the principal. An assistant principal or dean is probably in charge of substitute teachers and discipline.

Department heads and team leaders are good resources for questions about curriculum and can also offer advice on students. Guidance counselors and special education teachers are usually helpful when you have questions about students with behavior or learning problems that are not so serious they need to be referred to an administrator. Most students who have learning problems are in regular classes for a part of the day, but the resource room teacher probably knows them better than anyone else. Homeroom teachers or teacher advisors in many schools have special relationships with their students and can offer good advice.

Questions about audio-visual equipment and materials can be answered by the librarian or media specialist. For help with computers, see the computer specialist or another teacher.

The three best and usually most accessible resource people for your nitty gritty questions are the school secretaries, the custodians, and neighboring teachers. If you aren't sure about something, ask. A small detail can often escalate into a larger problem which might have been avoided if you had taken a minute to get someone's help in the beginning. People are usually flattered when they are asked for their advice so don't hesitate.

If you have any questions and you don't know whom to ask, check with the secretary. If she can't help you, she'll know who can. She's also the person to see about getting supplies or duplicating materials which you need.

SOME TIPS FOR CLASSROOM CONTROL: FOCUS ON PREVENTING PROBLEMS

*Act confident even though you don't feel that way.

*Use eye contact when speaking to the class or individual students. You can "tell" a student to stop drumming his fingers on the desk with a "Stop that!" glance while you continue the lesson.

*Make an effort to learn students' names as quickly as possible and then use them. Even though it's difficult to learn a lot of names all at once, you can give the illusion that you know more names that you actually do if you strategically place the seating chart where it's accessible to surreptitious glances. Identifying a potential troublemaker by name right away is a good move. Students appreciate someone who cares enough to learn who they are, and your knowing the names makes it more difficult for students to misbehave and get away with it. "Mike, please turn around" is much more effective than "You in the yellow shirt, turn around."

*Move around the room. If you are physically near students as you teach, they are less likely to be inattentive. You can also keep them off guard since they won't know exactly where you'll be at a given moment. When they have a writing or reading assignment to do, take a seat in the back row where they'll have to turn around to see you instead of sitting in front of the class at the teacher's desk.

*Involve as many students as possible in the class discussion. Don't let a few outgoing students answer all the questions or dominate the discussion. You can invite a reliable student to record a check next to the names of the students as they participate so you can tell who hasn't answered and call on them. This method can also be used by the teacher as an "oral quiz." Tell students the questions or discussion will be considered as a quiz. They must answer at least one question to pass. At the end of the session assign letter grades by looking at the number of checks individuals have earned by participating and making a scale for the class, e.g. 7-8 = A; 5-6 = B, etc. If during the discussion some students talk too much, put them "on hold" for a while so other students can talk and earn checks.

*If the lesson is question and answer, give the question BEFORE calling on anyone so all students will mentally prepare a response. If you call a student's name first, the others will breathe a sigh of relief and not pay attention until the next question. For the same reason don't call on students in order.

*Keep students busy for the whole period. When possible, have the instructions written on the board so students can end one task and begin another without disturbing other students. Any time there's a possibility students will finish a task before the rest of the class does, tell them ahead of time what they are to do when they finish.

*If work has to be written on the board during class, have a student do it rather than doing it yourself. That way you don't have to turn your back on the class and increase the possibility of problems developing.

*Allow students to work in groups or move freely around the room ONLY when you are sure you have the class well in control. You probably won't want to give any freedom to classes the first day you substitute for them unless the class needs to be up and around, such as in a home ec cooking lab, or working together in a writing workshop, for example. When you do allow students to work together establish a signal (such as flicking the lights) to use when the noise level gets too high and you want them to quiet down or return to their seats.

*Keep students from leaving the room unless absolutely necessary and then allow only one student out at a time. At the beginning of the class, tell students your policy is no leaving the room except for emergencies.

*Tell students in a study hall that no one will get a library pass or other privilege, such as working with another student, until attendance has been taken and everyone is working quietly.

*Give students specific directions before doing anything, even just passing in papers. Instead of saying, "Pass your papers in," which in some classes can create a free-for-all, say, "Pass the papers to the person in front of you. I will collect them from the first person in each row."

*When problems do occur, follow your plan and DON'T resort to any of the following:

●Threats you can't carry out. "You will all stay after school!" How will you enforce that? If you have the same students again, they'll remember your empty threats.

●Punishments which may create greater problems. "Write I will not chew gum 1000 times." Can the student finish in the time allowed? Does the punishment fit the crime? What will you do if the student refuses? It's not a good idea to use writing as punishment because you create negative attitudes about writing. Other school subjects are not treated this way. The English teacher wouldn't dream of saying, "Since you were late to class, you'll have to do 10 math problems."

•Ultimatums. "You do that once more, and you're going to the office." For throwing a wad of paper on the floor? What will you do if there's a fight? Are the two situations equally serious? What does sending students to the office say about your ability to control students?

•Punishing the whole class. You'll create more problems than you solve. Students don't think it's fair that they be punished for something someone else did. They're right. If the whole class is especially difficult to manage, ask the principal, department head, or team leader to drop in unannounced.

*Use positive statements to motivate students. "I wonder which row can finish first." "Who can write a better ending to this story?" "Can the students on the right side of the room get more right than those of you on the left?" "I'll bet no one can finish this assignment without making a mistake." "The first five people to finish cleaning up will be the first ones to leave for lunch (or recess)."

*Don't point at students or touch or grab them. Pointing seems like an attack to some students. You can be sued for using physical means for anything other than keeping a student from hurting himself or others. Actually you could get sued in that case, too, but if the judge believed your action was justified to prevent harm, you'd win the suit.

*Be understanding, firm, fair, and friendly. Say "Please" and "Thank you." Offer to help a student who's having trouble getting his/her locker open.

*Keep your sense of humor and use it. If the first student in the room growls at you and says, "I hate subs!" Smile and say, "I know how you feel. I hate dentists myself, but they're great when you've got a toothache." If unidentified students are making animal noises during class, don't waste your energy trying to search out the culprit(s). Smile and say, "I had no idea Old MacDonald's farm was so close by. I hope his animals will let us finish today's lesson. It'd be a shame if you had extra homework to do because we couldn't get it done in class." Students making such noises are trying to get your goat. If they see that the noises aren't going to accomplish their objective, they'll soon quit.

WHAT TO DO IF...

THE TEACHER DOESN'T LEAVE A SEATING PLAN

If you have time before students arrive, make a rough chart form of the way the desks are arranged. Then either choose a responsible student to fill in the names or pass it around the room and ask students to fill in their own names. If you don't trust students to put the right names down, give them a topic to write on and walk around the room filling in your chart with their names from their papers. If you tell them you'd like to know what fashions are currently in style, how they feel about some issue of concern to them, or their descriptions of the ideal teacher, they'll be willing to write and will automatically fill in the correct names on their papers. For insurance, tell them you'll collect the papers and tell the regular teacher to give them credit for doing the assignment.

THE TEACHER DOESN'T LEAVE ANY LESSON PLAN

Come prepared with activities of your own. See Chapter Six and Part II for ideas. Giving students a study period may be an invitation to disaster in many classes.

THE LESSON PLAN IS INCOMPLETE OR MATERIALS ARE MISSING

Improvise! A substitute teacher in a kindergarten class found the instructions, "Make lambs." However, there weren't enough cotton balls for everyone to make lambs, because each lamb would require several cotton balls, so she had the students make bunnies, requiring only one cotton ball for the tail of each child's bunny.

THE WHOLE CLASS MISBEHAVES

If you are completely unable from the beginning to deal effectively with a group of students despite your very best efforts, call on the principal (or whoever is in charge of discipline) for help. A teacher in a neighboring classroom who knows the students may be able to help as well. After the other person has brought the group under some control, you should be able to maintain it. If you are substituting in an elementary school where you can control the recess, you may be able to solve the problem by telling the students the time they waste now, they'll lose from recess.

SOMETHING HAPPENS AND NO ONE OWNS UP

This kind of situation occurs when something is stolen or damaged in the room. Sometimes there is no solution to the problem, but keep the students in the room and call in someone else to help. Don't dismiss the class even if the period has ended. Many times the students can be left by themselves after an administrator or another teacher has spoken to them, and the guilty party will own up. This technique will probably not work for you so don't attempt to handle the problem by yourself.

YOU SUSPECT A STUDENT IS INVOLVED WITH DRUGS OR ALCOHOL

Talk directly with the principal or assistant principal. Send a note with a student or ask on the intercom that someone come to your room. You should not leave the students unsupervised to go to the office yourself, and, depending on the student's condition, you probably shouldn't try to send the student there on his or her own. But if the latter does seem okay to do, send a separate note in a sealed envelope with another student explaining what's happened.

THE STUDENTS TELL YOU, "MR. JONES ALWAYS..."

The simple response is, "I'm not Mr. Jones, and this is what we'll do today" or, even better, "This will be a crazy day. Since I'm not Mr. Jones, I probably won't do everything the way he does. Let's have a contest. When I do something different, jot it down. At the end of the day we'll see who spotted the most differences." Of course, you can, with students' help, try to do as much as you can the way Mr. Jones would.

A FIGHT DEVELOPS

Get help immediately from a teacher in the next classroom and send a student to get an administrator. Use your best judgement about breaking up the fight. Do so if you can, but you should try to prevent harm to other students and yourself.

THERE'S A FIRE DRILL

Exit directions for your classroom should be posted in the room. Have students exit quickly and quietly following these directions. Close all windows and doors and turn off the lights. Be sure to take the teacher's gradebook or roll sheets with you since you may have to take attendance outside. If you are uncertain about where to go, follow the students or ask another teacher.

SOMEONE GETS HURT OR BECOMES ILL

Immediately contact the main office and the school nurse. Seek assistance from a teacher nearby if necessary. Check to see if you have to complete or sign an accident report.

YOU DON'T HAVE ENOUGH BACKGROUND IN THE SUBJECT MATTER TO TEACH STUDENTS

Don't try. Let students go over the material and check each other or have them do a writing assignment, such as summarizing the chapter in their own words. See Chapter Six.

SOME STUDENTS FINISH THE ASSIGNED WORK BEFORE OTHERS

Have an assignment written on the board (See Part II for ideas) or bring in magazines for them to read.

A CHANGE OF PACE IS CALLED FOR OR THE LESSON IS FINISHED AND THERE ARE STILL TEN MINUTES LEFT IN THE PERIOD

See Part II for puzzles and games you can play or bring in a story to read aloud.

A STUDENT BRINGS UP A SUBJECT YOU'RE NOT COMFORTABLE DISCUSSING, SUCH AS DEATH OR SEX

Listen, be accepting but refer the student to someone else, such as a guidance counselor, for further help.

STUDENTS HAVE LITTLE OR NOTHING TO SAY IN A CLASS DISCUSSION AFTER WATCHING A FILM OR READING A STORY

Give them a few minutes to write individual responses, reactions, and questions without worrying about spelling and mechanics. They can share these pieces by reading them or talking about them. See Chapter Six for more information.

THE PRINCIPAL VISITS YOUR CLASS

Don't worry! He or she probably just wants to make sure things are going okay. Keep right on with the lesson. If you do a good job, you'll have another person to use as a reference when you look for a fulltime job!

A LITTLE PRACTICE SUBSTITUTE TEACHING

Here is a brainstormed list of the kind of problems you're most likely to face in the classroom as a substitute teacher. Decide how you would prevent the situation or how you would deal with it if it did occur. If you're not sure, skim this chapter and Chapter Four again for suggestions. Remember that the best solution for some problems is doing nothing!

STUDENTS

sit in the wrong seats.

give the wrong names.

slam their books on the desk.

ask for passes to their lockers, the restroom, the guidance office, the gym, the main office, the library, or another classroom.

throw chalk, spitballs, wadded up paper, books, or pencils.

cough in unison or one right after the other in a chain.

talk while you're talking.

refuse to sit down.

move their desks or chairs without permission.

tap pencils or drum fingers on desks.

throw books out the window.

ask silly questions in the middle of a lesson.

play with classroom displays.

tease classroom animals or set them free.

take something that belongs to another student.

play with "toys."

eat candy or chew gum in class.

imitate someone from the office calling you on the intercom and get you to answer.

hum in unison when you turn the lights on and stop when you turn them off.

write notes to friends instead of doing the assignment.

draw unflattering pictures of you.

punch or poke another student.

yell out answers when you've told them to raise their hands.

tattle on classmates.

call classmates names.

all talk at once.

hand in blank papers.

get out of their seats to sharpen pencils while you're teaching.

swear in the classroom (but not at anyone).

swear at you.

do homework for another class instead of their assignment.

read in a sing-song way on purpose when reading a play or story aloud.

copy answers from another student's paper.

pretend they don't understand when you ask a question or explain something.

sleep in class.

daydream or doodle in class.

How did you do? The list above is about as bad as it will get. If you were able to figure out how you would handle the situations listed, you're all set to substitute. Admittedly, it will be a bit harder to deal with real students in a real classroom, but by thinking about what you would do ahead of time, there are few situations that can come up which you haven't already thought about. All you need is a little practice with real students. The more you get, the better you will be. Go for it!

Chapter Six

THINKING ABOUT WRITING IN NEW WAYS

WRITING no longer belongs only in the English and language arts classrooms. You'll find students doing writing assignments in every grade in every subject because many teachers are now using writing not only as a way to check on what students have or have not learned but also as a method for helping them learn.

Writing can be used like discussion and reading as a way of learning and understanding a chapter in a history book or a new concept in math. When students use writing in this way, teachers don't correct or grade most of the students' papers. You may find this fact surprising and perhaps feel that such teachers aren't doing the job they should. Consider though that teachers rarely assign letter grades to class discussions or reading assignments in the textbook nor do they stop a class discussion every time students make usage errors to correct them.

This chapter will be useful to you as a substitute teacher because it will provide you with information for using writing in a variety of ways in the classroom. Writing can be especially useful when the teacher doesn't leave any lesson plans, when you want to vary the activities during the class period, when you want to solve problems with a class or an individual student, and when you'd like student feedback on your effectiveness as a substitute teacher.

WRITING TO EVALUATE

You are already very familiar with writing when it's used as a means of evaluation. Teachers read, correct, and grade student writing in many classes. They determine what students have learned in a science or social studies unit by giving them essay tests or they evaluate how well students in an English class have understood a poem by having them write a critical essay. Most of the writing you did when you were in school was probably writing from which the teacher could assess what you already knew or didn't know about a subject.

Teaching Writing as a Process

One difference you may find in the way students work on writing to be evaluated in English or language arts classrooms these days is the process students go through to produce a paper which the teacher will grade. Few teachers assign an essay topic and leave the students to complete the assignment on their own to be handed in as a final copy on the due date.

Instead teachers first spend time in class having students do prewriting activities: brainstorming ideas for their papers, making clusters (visual brainstorming--beginning with the topic written in a circle in the middle of a page, students list related ideas in circles, connecting them to each other with lines. See the illustration for a concept map in Chapter Eight.), talking about their ideas with other students in small groups, role playing, or watching a film.

Then students write rough drafts which they bring into class. Sometimes the teacher collects and reads these drafts, but more often students read them to each other in pairs or small groups. As the other students comment and ask questions on a draft which has been read, the author makes notes of changes to make. The teacher may hold individual conferences with students. At this point no one worries about spelling, mechanics, and other surface features of the writing. In the drafting and revising stage, students focus on getting their ideas down on paper, developing them in some depth, making them clear, and presenting them in an organized fashion. Some students will write several drafts for the same assignment before they feel their pieces are ready for final drafts. Throughout the process students work with the teacher and with each other. The classroom becomes a writing workshop.

When their pieces are ready for editing, students again work with each other to check spelling, punctuation, sentence structure and the like, correcting errors they discover. Then they make neat final copies of their pieces to hand in to the teacher to be graded or published. Because teachers have realized the motivational and instructional benefits of having students write for other audiences in addition to the teacher, students may write pieces which they "publish" on the bulletin board, in a class magazine or newsletter, send to the local newspaper or enter in a writing contest in addition to those that teachers correct and grade.

Students in the primary grades are often allowed to write their stories with invented spelling, i.e. they sound the word out and write down the letters they think the word has. Primary teachers become experts at deciphering these individualistic spellings. Because these young students are not yet able to edit their own work (although they do revise what they write), parent volunteers or aides type their final pieces with conventional spelling and punctuation. Then the stories are bound into books and added to the classroom library for other students to read. As they do more reading and writing, the children gradually begin to use standard spelling so that most children no longer use invented spelling after second grade.

You'll probably find charts which list the steps of the writing process as described above in many classrooms:

Prewriting

Drafting

Revising

Editing

Publishing

In most cases when you find these charts posted in the room, you'll know that the teacher spends a lot of class time helping students with their writing and the students are encouraged to help each other. If the lesson plan says that students are to work on their writing, the teacher probably expects that you will allow them to work with each other.

WRITING TO LEARN

Writing to learn is a way of helping students process new information by talking or thinking paper. When students summarize new information in their own words, they remember it longer. It's been estimated that we remember 10 percent of what we read, 20 percent of what we hear, 30 percent of what we see, and 70 percent of what we ourselves say. There's no way a teacher can have everyone talk through the new material in a typical class. There just wouldn't be time, given the number of students in the class. Writing then becomes a way of "talking" on paper.

Consider how a writing-to-learn activity can increase the amount of learning that occurs when students read an assigned chapter in a social studies text. A typical traditional assignment would be to write out the answers to the questions at the end of the chapter. What usually happens? Many students don't even read the chapter. Instead they read the question, flip back through the chapter, checking the topic headings until they find the one they need, and then copy the textbook words onto their papers. It's possible for a student to write complete answers to all of the questions without ever thinking about one idea in the chapter. The student has the assignment ready the next day, the teacher is pleased, but the student has learned nothing! This fact may be apparent if the teacher gives a surprise quiz over the material.

On the other hand, if the teacher asks students to write summaries of the important information in the chapter (in their own words), students are forced to think about the material, process it, and decide what information has the greatest importance. In class the next day the teacher may ask students to read their summaries to classmates in small groups, discuss them, and then choose the best one. All of this processing of the information will help students understand and remember it in ways traditional assignments will not. Of course, there's an additional benefit, too: students are getting valuable practice in thinking and writing while they are studying a particular topic.

Because writing-to-learn is considered a means of comprehending and remembering information and not a learning-to-write assignment, teachers tell students not to worry about spelling, mechanics, and sentence structure. Their purpose is to get their ideas down on paper. Of course, a teacher may ask that students revise and polish a piece that was originally done as a writing-to-learn activity, make a final copy, and turn it in for a grade. Usually, however, this kind of writing is for the students' benefit in learning content so the teacher may check to see that papers have been done but will not correct or grade them.

Because teachers can get a great deal of information from these papers which helps them do a better job, they often do quick reading as a means of checking on their own teaching. If students spend the last five minutes of the class summarizing what they have learned in a learning log, the teacher can tell how well the students understood the new material, what confusion still exists, and what, if anything, needs to be retaught the next day. Because every student did a learning log, they know how everyone is doing. It may appear that the class understands the new material when the teacher questions students orally, but only a few students may be doing most of the responding.

A Sampling of
Writing-To-Learn Activities

These activities can be adapted for use in any class at any level in any subject. When you ask students to write, tell them, not to worry about spelling and mechanics. The exercises are for "thinking or talking on paper."

After students finish writing, you have several options: collect the papers to read later, ask volunteers to share what they wrote and then collect, have students share with one other student or in small groups and then collect, or after sharing, let students keep papers for themselves, the way they would keep notes they took in class.

*Write down everything you know about [topic which has been studied or is about to be studied]. When students write all they know about a subject before they study it, teachers can clear up prior misunderstandings which could hinder or obstruct the new learning if they went unnoticed and uncorrected.

*Write down what you think will happen next. Students can write what they think a character in a story will do next or where a particular event they've been studying in history might lead. Then they read to see how accurate their predictions were.

*Paraphrase the text or lecture or write a summary in your own words.

*Write down all the questions you'd like answered about this chapter (or topic).

*Write a summary of today's lesson for a student who was absent. If a new math concept is taught, students write explaining how that concept works or the process they would use to solve a problem.

*Write your reactions to [the film, lecture, class activity, or reading assignment].

*Write how you think this [chapter, story, concept] applies to your life.

*Write a dialogue [between two characters in the story or from two different stories, two historical characters, two math symbols].

*Write a letter to the author of your textbook.

*Summarize what you have learned in this class [today, this week, this month, this semester].

*Write out solutions to problems.

*Respond to situations.

WRITING TO COMMUNICATE

Writing also offers the teacher, and you as a substitute, a way of finding out what students think. Give students an opportunity to talk to you on paper. You can learn more about individual students and get valuable information to help you do a better job as a teacher.

When you ask students to do this kind of writing, call it a "free writing," i.e. they are free from worrying about mechanics and form. Free writings are a good way of using the few minutes of wasted or dead time at the beginning or end of the class. You'll find it very enjoyable to get to know some of your students, something that's usually not possible when you are covering a class just for the day.

Here are some ways you might want to use free writings when you substitute.

*Tell me about yourself and what you've been learning in this class. This is a good topic for the beginning of the class when you first take over.

*What did you think of today's activity? What changes should I make when I do it the next time? This information is very useful when you try out activities from your own survival kit. Even if students write only about what was wrong with the activity, as you read their comments, you may be able to figure out how to avoid the problem the next time.

*Tell me how you think I did as a sub today. What did I do well? What do I need to work on? Of course, this topic is risky, but subs usually get no feedback on their teaching. Students generally will be thoughtful and honest in their responses. Disregard the totally negative and insensitive ones. You may be surprised, however, at how much positive feedback you get.

*Tell me why you were late to class.

*Tell me why you weren't able to finish your homework today.

*We can't continue with the discussion if everyone is going to talk at once. Tell me how you think we might solve this problem. Having them all write will quiet the class down. Have them share their ideas. The problem may be solved without your doing anything else.

*I'd like each of you to write down what happened. This technique is very useful when two students are squabbling with each other or there has been some other problem between two students. When they finish, have each listen while the other reads what he/she has written. Then ask both how they might resolve the issue.

There are many, many ways to use writing in any classroom. This chapter has given you a few beginning ideas. Try these, adapt them, and/or experiment with ideas of your own. Chances are, when you're stuck and can't figure out what to do next, asking students to write will lead to a solution. Sometimes the act of writing itself turns out to be the solution. You'll find that writing can be a powerful and effective tool for substitute teachers.

PART TWO

ACTIVITIES AND ASSIGNMENTS

PREFACE

EVEN THOUGH the activities here have been categorized by level and subject, you'll get the most benefit by skimming all of the activities described. Many activities listed for elementary students will work with older students and vice-versa. Especially in the English/ Language Arts section of Chapter Six, you'll find activities that you can do with students of many ages in any subject if you find yourself without any lesson plan or materials.

As you read the activities, note the ones that sound interesting or useful to you. Later you can make up class sets of handouts to put in your substitute survival kit. To save paper and extra work, make enough copies of handouts for one class (Thirty-five should cover most classes.) Number the handouts # 1-35, saving a few extra copies to replace those which get lost or damaged. When you use the handouts with a class, ask students to write their responses on another sheet. Collect the handouts, put them back in numerical order, and they're ready to use again.

Put photos or other materials you collect to pass around a class in plastic protectors or mount them on oaktag or thin cardboard and cover with a transparent, self-stick plastic covering.

After you try an activity, jot down notes about how it went and what you need to do or remember the next time so that things will go more smoothly. Save these notes in the folder with the handouts for that activity. Don't discard an idea just because it didn't go well the first time. Perhaps it was too difficult for a particular group of students, but it might be perfect for your next class.

Over time you'll acquire a sizeable number of resources to use when you sub. You'll never have to worry about finding yourself in a classroom with no plans, no books, and nothing to do. You'll be ready for almost any situation.

Chapter Seven

ELEMENTARY ACTIVITIES

(Kindergarten to Grade Six)

BOOKS AND STORIES TO READ ALOUD

ACCORDING to Jim Trelease, the author of *The Read-Aloud Handbook* (a book you should own if you have young children or plan to substitute in the elementary grades on a regular basis), a good read-aloud book should (1) hook the child into the plot as soon as possible (2) have clear, rounded characters (3) contain crisp, easy-to-read dialogue and (4) keep long descriptive passages to a minimum at least in the beginning.

Trelease's book contains an extensive list of read-aloud books for all ages along with brief descriptions of each. The following titles--just a sampling--have been recommended by Trelease and also appear on other lists of recommended books for children. You should be able to find most of them in a library near you. Some can be purchased in inexpensive paperback editions. Suggested grade levels appear in parentheses after each entry.

Your local children's librarian can recommend other good books. You should read the books yourself before you attempt to read them to students. If you have copies of your own favorites, take them with you when you sub. A good story never gets boring, and children love to read and hear their favorite stories over and over and over.

The picture books can be easily read if you have the students for only one day. The short novels you might want to keep in mind when you'll be with the same class for several days. Longer novels aren't listed because unless you're hired as a long-term sub, you'll never have enough time to finish them. Of course, reading the beginning of a novel aloud to older children is a good way to motivate them to check the book out of the library and finish reading it themselves.

Picture Books

Alexander and the Terrible, Horrible, No Good, Very Bad Day by Judith Viorst (K up) This book can also be read to teenagers as a springboard for writing about their own bad days.
Amelia Bedelia (and other books in the series) by Peggy Parrish (K-4)
The Bear's Toothache by David McPhail (Pre-K to 2)
Bedtime for Frances by Russell Hoban (Pre-K to 2)
Bennett Cerf's Book of Animal Riddles by Bennett Cerf (Pre-K to 2)
Blueberries for Sal by Robert McCloskey (Pre-K to K)
The Book of Giant Stories by David Harrison (K-3)
Cloudy with a Chance of Meatballs by Judi Barrett (K-5)
Corduroy by Don Freeman (Pre-K to 2)
Cranberry Thanksgiving by Wende and Harry Devlin (K-4)
Don't Forget the Bacon by Pat Hutchins (K-5)
Fables by Arnold Lobel (2-6)
The Giving Tree by Shel Silverstein (also other books by this author)(K-4)
The Great Hamster Hunt by Lenore Blegvad and Erik Blegvad (K-3)
Hans Andersen-His Classic Fairy Tales Translated by Erik Haugaard (K up)
Household Stories of the Brothers Grimm Translated by Lucy Crane (K up)
Ira Sleeps Over by Bernard Waber (K-6)
The Leatherman by Dick Gackenbach (2-5)
Madeline by Ludwig Bemelmans (and other books in the series) (Pre-K to 2)
Make Way for Ducklings by Robert McCloskey (Pre-K to 2)
Miss Nelson Is Missing by Harry Allard (Pre-K to 4)
Mother Goose, A Treasury of Best-Loved Rhymes Edited by Watty Piper)Pre-K to 2)
My Grandson Lew by Charlotte Zolotow (K-6)
No Boys Allowed by Susan Terris (K-5)
Prince of the Dolomites by Tomie de Paola (1-5)
Sam, Bangs and Moonshine by Evaline Ness (1-4)
Sarah's Unicorn by Bruce and Katherine Coville (K-2)
Sleep Out by Carol Carrick (K-5)
The Stupids Step Out by Harry Allard (1-4)
The Sweet Tooth by Lorna Balian (K-5)
Sylvester and the Magic Pebble by William Steig (Pre-K to 4)

The Tale of Peter Rabbit by Beatrix Potter (Pre-K to 1)
The Tenth Good Thing about Barney by Judith Viorst (K-6)
That Terrible Halloween Night by James Stevenson (Pre-K to 4)
Tintin in Tibet (and other books in the series) by Herge (2-4)
Wolfie by Janet Cheney (K-2)
You Ought To See Herbert's House by Doris Lund (K-4)

Short Novels

Among the Dolls by William Sleator (4-6)
The Best Christmas Pageant Ever by Barbara Robinson (2-6)
Call It Courage by Armstrong Sperry (2-6)
Chocolate Fever by Robert K. Smith (1-5)
Dexter by Clyde Robert Bulla (2-5)
Family Secret: Five Very Important Stories by Norma Shreve (3-7)
Freckle Juice by Judy Blume (2-5)
The Gumdrop Necklace by Phyllis LaFarge (2-5)
Help! I'm a Prisoner in the Library by Eth Clifford
The Hundred Dresses by Eleanor Estes (3-6)
The Leopard's Tooth by William Kotzwinkle (5-7)
The Littles by John Peterson (1-4)
The Magic Finger by Roald Dahl (2-6)
My Father's Dragon by Ruth S. Gannett
The Real Thief by William Steig (3-5)
Room 10 by Agnes McCarthy (1-4)
Soup by Robert Newton Peck (4-6)
Storm Boy by Colin Thiele (3-6)
A Taste of Blackberries by Doris B. Smith (4-7)
Twenty and Ten by Claire H. Bishop (3-6)
Wigger by William Goldman (1-5)
The Witch of Fourth Street by Myron Levoy (2-5)

FIFTY ACTIVITIES FOR YOUNG STUDENTS

1. Consonant Pictures (1-2)

Have each child draw something in the room whose name begins with a consonant sound. You may wish to provide a list of consonants on the board. Then have children show their finished pictures to the class and have others guess what consonant sound each child has pictured.

2. Listen Up (1-3)

Write three to five familiar words on the board. Children should have paper and pencils ready as you read aloud a sentence which includes all of the words on the board except one. They are to write down the missing word.

3. Phonics Guessing Game (1-2)

You say, "I am thinking of an object in this room which begins with the 'b' sound. What is it?" The child who gets the right answer then gets to select the next object for the others to guess.

4. Letter Bingo (1-3)

Make up bingo cards with consonant sounds instead of numbers. Play the game the same way as you would regular bingo except you call out words instead of numbers and children cover the beginning sounds on their cards.

5. Word Search (1 up)

Write any word on the board and have students find as many small words in the large word as they can. You can use ordinary words, holiday words, the school name, or your name. Older students can handle more difficult words and may also be asked to write words that can be made by using the letters from the original word in any order in addtion to the small words that already appear within the original word.

6. Riddles (1 up)

Make up simple riddles by giving clues about objects in the room. "I help you do your school work. I am flat. I have a smooth surface. Etc. What am I?" (Desk) Begin with one or two clues and add more if necessary. For a variation have students write their own riddles for others to guess.

7. Rhyming (1 up)

"What rhymes with [You fill in a word]?" Have students list as many rhyming words as they can think of.

8. Vowel Substitute (1-3)

Write a simple word on the board, such as **sat**. Have students write as many words as they can by substituting other vowels for the one in the original word.

9. Vowel Recognition (1-4)

Have children all stand by their desks. Say a word with a long or short vowel. If students hear a short vowel, they put their hands on top of their heads; if they hear a long vowel, they raise their hands straight up in the air. Students with the correct answer remain standing; the others sit down. The winner is the last student standing.

10. Name Mix-Up (2-4)

Write the names of the students in the class on the board, but mix up the order of the letters. Students write the names correctly. You can do the names one at a time for students to write on their papers or on the board. If you choose to do the exercise on the board, the student who writes the name correctly gets to write the next name (perhaps with your help) mixed up for the others to guess.

11. Word Hunt (2 up)

Give students a photocopied story from a book or newspaper. Say a word which appears one or more times in the story. Students are to circle it every time it appears. Continue with other words. Older students can be given more difficult words to look for. You may wish to number the lines of the text so that it is easy to identify where the words appear.

12. Scrambled Syllables (2 up)

Write multi-syllable words on the board with the syllables written in the wrong order. Students write the scrambled words correctly. Older students can be given a scrambled phrase or common saying instead of just one word to figure out.

13. Words in Code (2 up)

Make up a code with a symbol representing each letter, e.g. & = A; $ = S, etc. Then write words or sentences using the code for students to decipher. Example: &$ = AS. Younger children can do simple words, one at a time; older students can figure out messages of a sentence or two. A variation for older students is to let them make up their own codes and messages for others in the class to decipher. (Codes can also be created by using the Cyrillac alphabet letters the Greeks and Russians use and then writing English words phonetically with the new alphabet. You can find this alphabet in many large dictionaries.)

14. Scrambled Sentences (2 up)

The teacher or the students write sentences in scrambled order for the others in the class to unscramble. Older students can be given paragraphs with sentences in the wrong order to rewrite. You may wish to duplicate a short story or essay and cut it in pieces for students working in pairs or small groups to reconstruct correctly.

15. Add a Letter (3 up)

Write a word on the board. Students are to make a new word or words by adding only one letter to the original.

16. Fill-in-the-Blank Story (2 up)

Write a simple story, leaving blanks for the children to fill in as they wish. "Once there was a child named _____ . The child lived _____ and more than anything wanted _____ . Etc." Children read their finished stories to each other.

17. Write Your Own Ending (2 up)

Read a story to the class but stop before reading the ending. Let students tell or write their own endings to the story and share them with each other.

18. Ghost Writing (3 up)

One child comes to the board and "writes" a word by using the correct motions but without actually writing anything on the board. The child who guesses the word that has been written by the ghost gets to "write" the next word.

19. Class Story (2 up)

One student begins the story by giving one word. The next child adds a word to continue and so on. Students are "out" if the word they choose will not gramatically fit the words already there. A variation for older students is to have the first student give the first sentence of the story. The second student adds the second sentence and so on.

20. Word Chain (2 up)

Write a word on the board. Students write as many words as they can think of that begin with the last letter of the word on the board. A variation is writing a word for each letter of the alphabet.

21. Category Game (3 up)

Write a general category on the board, such as sports. Have students write as many words as they can which fit that category. A variation (and similar to a popular board game) is to make up cards with a number of letters (common ones only) and others with general categories. Draw five letters and one to five category cards. Students compete within a given time to fill in one word which begins with the appropriate letter for each category so selected. They write their answers down in chart form.

Letters Drawn	Category: Sports
B	Baseball
T	Tennis
R	Racketball
V	Volleyball
R	Football

22. Spelling Bee with Variations (3 up)

Spelling bees can be conducted in the normal way or with modification. For example, simple math problems to solve can be substituted for words to spell or students can be asked to give a synonym, antonym, or rhyming word for a word instead of spelling it. If students are reviewing a history or science topic, the teacher can ask review questions. Students remain standing as long as they answer correctly. Another way to make the spelling bee more challenging is to have students spell the words backwards!

23. Name Poems (3 up)

Write the child's name (school name or other topic for a poem, such as winter) on the board vertically. Students then use the first letter on each line as the beginning of a word or phrase that describes the subject of the poem. Students can write two or three words on each line, but only the first word needs to begin with the designated letter. Encourage students to use descriptive rather than general words so that the reader gets a mental picture from reading the finished poem.

Cats

Cuddly, soft and warm
Animals to snuggle and play with
The best friends for telling secrets to
Silly and playful when they aren't sleeping

24. Think Verbs (4 up)

Write a noun on the board, such as **cat**. Students write as many verbs as they can think of that can go with that noun. Examples: **eat, run, pounce, scratch, bite, purr,** etc.

25. Memory Game (4 up)

The first student gives a word beginning with "a," the second with "b," etc. Each student must repeat correctly and in order the words the students before have already given before adding a new one. This game gets very challenging! The teacher should write the words down as they are added so that there is an accurate list should a challenge occur.

26. Numbers and Shapes (1-2)

Draw a circle, triangle, square, etc. on the board. Put a number inside each shape. Ask children to draw Shape # 1 or, more of a challenge, draw the shape number which comes after (or before) # 1.

27. How Many? (1-2)

The teacher says, "I see some yellow objects on the window sill" or "white sweaters in the first row." "How many do I see?" Children write down or say aloud the number they see.

28. Number Team Contest (1-2)

Group the students into equal teams and have them all stand in rows. Tell students to listen and after you say, "Go," they are to follow the directions you have given as quickly as they can. Give directions for the first person in each row to put their hands on their heads, the fourth person to..., etc. Mix the order up. Then say, "Go." The first team to finish doing what you have directed wins.

29. Number Problem Bingo (2 up)

Instead of giving letters and numbers for Bingo the regular way, give students a simple problem. For example, cover the number for 1 plus 1. Students would cover 2. Problems for older students can be made more challenging.

30. Count the Claps (1-2)

Have students write down the number of times they hear you clap. The winner gets to do the clapping for the next set.

31. Number Name Game (1-3)

Give each child in the class a single-digit number (use the same number for several children if necessary). Write the names with their numbers on the board. You then say, "Add Tom to Jane." "Subtract Toby." Etc. The first child with the correct numerical answer when you finish wins.

32. Number Squares (2-4)

Have each child make a double set of number squares for the numbers 1-9. You write a number on the board. Using their squares, students figure out a combination of numbers which would make the number on the board. They should try to come up with a combination no one else will think of. You may vary the game and make it more challenging by saying, "What numbers will make the number on the board if you can't use X?"

33. Mental Math (2 up)

You give simple math problems that students can figure in their heads, but give them in a series. Example: Add 2 and 3. Subtract 1. Add 10. Subtract 5. Etc. At the end ask, "What have you got?" To get the right answer, the students must not only be able to do the math, they must also pay attention!

34. Coin Combos (2-4)

Put a sum on the board. Ask students to list all of the combinations of coins that can make up that sum.

35. What Can I Buy? (2 up)

Cut out some store ads and photocopy or make a list of items children might want to purchase (toys, food, etc.) with their prices. Give them varying amounts of money to spend. Have them figure out what they would buy with each amount. You can vary this by asking what they would buy for someone else--a friend, a parent, or sibling. Another variation is to give them a list of items with larger purchase prices and ask them to figure out how long they would have to save to get X if they had $1 per week. You can use grocery ads to teach nutrition by having them "purchase" food for one day of balanced meals.

36. Measurement Mystery (4-5)

One student is chosen to measure an object of his or her choice while the other students close their eyes. The child then announces the size (length, width, height, etc.) to the class and they try to guess what object has been measured. The child who guesses first gets to choose the next object.

37. Decimal Line-Up (5-6)

One student lists a number of decimals on the board in random order: .249, .3, .1, .02, etc. The other students compete to see who can put them in the correct order--largest to smallest--first. As a variation, do the same thing with fractions.

38. Three-Way Switch (5-6)

You write a percentage, fraction or decimal on the board. Students then write the alternate forms of that same number. Example: 10 percent .1 1/10

39. Code Math (5-6)

On the board write the numbers 0-9 with codes for each number. Example 0 = $, 1 = *, etc. Then give students problems to solve in code or have them develop their own codes and write problems for classmates to solve.

40. Guessing Game (5-6)

Name an object in the room. Have students guess how tall or wide it is. They write down their estimates. Then a student actually measures the object and reports the answer. The student with the best estimate wins and gets to select the next object and do the measuring.

41. Number Story Problems (2 up)

Have students write their own number story problems. Younger students will write simpler ones while older students will probably want to stump their classmates. Students can form teams and compete with each other to solve the problems.

42. Travel Game (3 up)

Give each student a copy of a map of the United States. You give directions and ask questions to which they can call out or write down the responses. Example: You are in Boston and plan to go to Hartford. In what direction will you travel? To what state? Older students can be asked more difficult questions.

43. Greeting Cards (1 up)

Even though it's not any special holiday, students can create their own "Have a nice day" or "Thinking of you" cards to give to parents or friends. You can help younger children with the captions. Any form--from crayon or watercolor pictures or collage--can be the basis for the card.

44. Mystery Bag (1 up)

Put one or several objects in a bag. Have students reach in and feel what they are like. They may then write down what they think the object is, what it is most like, or how it feels. Older students will write more than younger ones. After everyone has guessed and/or written about what they discovered in the bag, you can display the objects. A variation: have students write a story based on one or all of the objects they think are in the bag.

45. Following Directions (1 up)

Give (or have students take turns giving) directions for students to draw simple shapes or designs on their papers. You (or the student) should draw the shape or design first and then write directions for reproducing it. Students follow the oral directions and do not see the original drawing until they finish. Students then compare what they have with what should have resulted. Older students who can write directions to give other students will learn how to give better directions as well as follow them from this activity.

46. Party Time (3 up)

Bring in some recipes for party foods. Have students double or triple the ingredients to make enough food for a party.

47. Comparisons (1 up)

Give students two objects or pictures to compare. They write or talk about what's the same and what's different about the objects.

48. Map Game (2 up)

Make copies of a local map and give one to each student. Ask them to locate various places or mark the shortest routes from point A to B on the map. You can make the activity into a scavenger hunt, i.e. students respond to a series of questions which can be answered by referring to the map. First student or team finished with the right answers wins.

49. Dictionary Scavenger Hunt (3 up)

Students form teams and respond to a series of questions whose answers can be found in the dictionary. You can do this same activity using an encyclopedia, textbooks, or other books and magazines in the room.

50. Categories (1 up)

Bring in a number of objects (or for older students write them on cards). Have students as individuals, pairs, or teams put them into categories and explain on what basis they are grouping objects together. Students will see that because categories are artificial creations, a given object may fit in a number of categories.

Chapter Eight

SECONDARY ACTIVITIES

(Grades Six to Twelve)

ENGLISH/LANGUAGE ARTS

Parts of Speech with Nonsense Words

CAN YOU TELL what part of speech each capitalized nonsense word is?

1. A GROOGY SPLOOK OOGLED into the room.
2. When I PIGGLED my GROOD, CASPENT GURPED.
3. He was SPADDLING CURNINGLY.
4. John is a GRADAT.
5. Susan GROND Judy talked GROND swam
6. A RAGNAT threw his TANEG to GLOOPER.
7. How SNIFFY the SLOOK was!
8. Bradbury swallowed some KROOP.
9. ZUMAS stroked his CHATSUM.
10. HITAS lowered the OMU.
11. Jean gave me an IGGIE and a TRIF.
12. CRUNCHIT left by PLOOPSIT.

Answer Key

1. Adjective/noun/verb
2. Verb/noun/noun/verb
3. Verb/adverb
4. Noun
5. Conjunction/conjunction
6. Noun/noun/noun

81

7. Adjective/noun
8. Noun
9. Noun/noun
10. Noun/noun
11. Noun/noun
12. Noun/noun

Follow-Up

1. Have students make up definitions for the nonsense words.
2. Have students make up nonsense words of their own and ask class-mates to label the parts of speech and write definitions for them.

Sentence Beginnings

There are many ways to begin sentences. Good writers aim for va-riety. Write sentences of your own using the following examples as models.

(Adverb) FINALLY she went home.

(Prepositional phrase) AT TEN O'CLOCK she went home.

(Participial phrase) NOT WANTING TO BE LATE, she hurried home.

(Inifinitive phrase) TO AVOID BEING LATE, she left in a hurry.

(Introductory dependent clause) BECAUSE SHE WAS LATE, she hur-ried home.

Alphabet Story

Have students write a story that follows the alphabet, i.e. the first word begins with a, the second with b, and so on. Students can write these individually or as a class with each student adding the next word in turn.

Sample Beginnings: A brave chicken desperately ...

A boring child disappointed ...

Anna brought candles despite ...

Multiple Meanings

Read the sample word and sentences for it and then write sentences for the other words listed. Each sentence should illustrate a different meaning for the word. Finding three different meanings for each word is the minimum. You should be able to come up with more. You may include slang meanings and change the part of speech or the ending of the word.

Sample: CAT

>The dog chased the CAT up a tree.
>
>The man crossed the canyon on a CATwalk.
>
>The landlady was an old CAT.
>
>Tom has a summer job driving a CAT.
>
>The CATS began to dig the beat. (old slang meaning)

1. CUT
2. SPRING
3. CAST
4. COOL
5. CROSS
6. BURN
7. WEED
8. RAT
9. BOOK
10. SQUARE

Possible Responses

1. CUT the bread.
   That was an unkind CUT.
   He CUT me down.
   Tim was CUT from the team.
   Mark CUT 5 classes last week.
   Please CUT the cards.
   Ken won the CUT in the card game.
   He took a shortCUT.
   The wind CUT through his coat.
2. SPRING is the best season.
   The SPRING in the car was broken.
   Weeds will SPRING up anywhere.
   The cat will SPRING from the shadows
   The bear will SPRING the trap.
   The water came from a SPRING.
3. The CAST on his leg is dirty.
   The CAST of the play rehearsed late.
   CAST your line into the stream.
   CAST your vote.
   CAST off your coat.

4. COOL weather comes in the fall.
   That guy is really COOL.
   She acted COOL towards me.
   Don't lose your COOL.
   The soup needs to COOL off.
   The man lost a COOL thousand.
   The man was thrown into the COOLER.
   The door was left open on the meat COOLER.

5. CROSS the river.
   He burned a CROSS.
   Mark the ballot with a CROSS.
   The teacher was CROSS.
   The child was CROSSeyed.
   He wanted to CROSS a lion with a tiger.

6. I was BURNed up.
   The BURN was severe.
   They BURNED the field.
   He had sideBURNS.
   She got a sunBURN.
   The BURNed house was razed.

7. Stop smoking WEEDS.
   WEEDS grow better than flowers.
   WEED out the poor students.
   She WEEDed the garden.
   She was wearing widow's WEEDS.

8. He's a RAT.
   She'd better not RAT on me.
   The cat left a dead RAT at the door.
   That is a RATty tie.
   She used a RATtail comb.

9. He was an open BOOK.
   The BOOK maker took bets.
   He BOOKED passage on the boat.
   He was a BOOKworm.
   I made BOOK on that last hand.
   Did you read the BOOK?
   The police BOOKED the man.

10. He drew a SQUARE.
    He lived near the town SQUARE.

The theory does not always SQUARE with the facts.
Her father is really SQUARE.
The boxers SQUARED off.

Sentence Variety

Here is an exercise which will help students write both longer and more varied sentences. Give them a series of short sentences about the same subject. Ask them to combine the information into one sentence, writing each sentence as many different ways as they can.
Example: His name was Sam. He had a brown dog. The dog chased cars. Sam was afraid.
Some Possible Responses: Sam was afraid because his brown dog chased cars.

Since his brown dog chased cars, Sam was afraid.

Sam's dog, who was brown, chased cars, causing Sam to be afraid.

Sam's brown dog chasing cars made him afraid.

Writing a Hundred-Word Sentence

Show students how they can add phrases and clauses to a simple sentence to make it longer and more complex. Then ask them to write a sentence with at least one hundred words. The sentence must not be a run-on and must make sense. Listing to get more words is not allowed. (I went to the store and bought bread, milk, eggs, bananas, ice cream, etc.) Sample: **The children playing on the front porch of the old house were surprised and even a bit frightened when all at once the wind came up, blowing leaves and branches off the trees, scattering flower petals all over the lawn, grabbing the towels drying on the clothesline and setting them free to fly around the yard until they finally came to rest in clumps here and there on the grass, and then heavy rain sheeted the windows and pelted the ground, flattened fragile plants and formed deep puddles everywhere, but just minutes later the sun shone brightly, the wet ground sparkled, and a rainbow formed in a now-clear sky.**

Show, Don't Tell Sentences

Good writers show rather than tell. Give students practice in writing with specifics by having them rewrite general statements with concrete details.

Example: He was nervous. Rewritten: He squirmed in his seat.

She was happy. Rewritten: She smiled even when the teacher snapped at her.

The girl was upset. Rewritten: Pretending to blow her nose, she cried softly into a wadded up tissue.

Writing Obituaries and Résumés

This excercise will give students practice writing in different forms at the same time they review their knowledge of literature. Have them write obituaries for literary characters or pretend that the literary character is applying for a job and put together a résumé for him/her.

Made-Up Book Titles

Have students brainstorm imaginary titles of books they'd like to read. Then have them each choose a different one and write a brief review of the book. Students can share their titles, let classmates guess what the books will be about, and then read the reviews they have written.

Plot in a Sentence

Have students think of plots for short stories and then summarize the plot in one sentence.
Example: Justin, who is twelve years old, carefree, careless, and somewhat irresponsible, finally convinces his parents to let him get the puppy he's wanted for a long time, but he forgets to shut the door when he dashes out to school, and the dog gets hit by a car.

Writing Anecdotes for *Reader's Digest*

Have students write anecdotes from their own experiences like the ones in the *Reader's Digest* column, "Life in These United States." If they come up with some good ones, encourage them to submit them to the magazine.
Example: "My father had trained his small poodle to fetch the newspaper. For six consecutive days he let her out the back door. Off she would go to the front of the house, trotting back proudly with her prize. On the seventh day she returned empty-mouthed with a hangdog expression.

Dad went to investigate and quickly realized the reason for her failure; he had sent his little poodle for the Sunday paper." (Angie Hamer, Longboat Key, Fla. in the July 1988 issue of *Reader's Digest*)

Writing Recipes

Using the standard recipe form for baking a cake or making cookies, have students write recipes for such things as doing well in school, getting along with parents, or making new friends.

Rules for Doing the Opposite

Writing with tongue in cheek is a lot of fun. Have students make up rules for getting an A in math, pleasing their parents, or getting along with friends, but instead of telling what would really accomplish those objectives, they write down the opposite.

Example: Rules for Getting an A in Math

1. Skip the homework once in a while so the teacher won't think you're compulsive.
2. Since two heads are better than one, get help on your test from a friend.
3. Make sure your papers look messy and somewhat hard to read. That way the teacher can tell that you spent all of your energy thinking about the problems instead of wasting time worrying about neatness. And so on.

Literary Dialogues

Have students take characters from two different stories or novels, imagine a situation where they might meet, and then write what they would say to each other.

Chain Story Writing

Have each student begin writing a story from a starter you give, such as, "The trouble really began when ..." After they have written for about three minutes, have them pass their papers to the students behind them. For the next three minutes, they continue adding to the stories they now have. Exchange papers again once or twice. Then direct students to write endings for the stories they now have. Read the stories aloud.

Personification Riddles

Students choose an inanimate object in the room, such as a pencil, desk, or textbook, and write a piece (either prose or poetry) pretending they are the objects chosen. Short sample: "I hate it when people chew on me and leave my smooth yellow skin full of pock marks. They don't appreciate all the work I do." (a pencil) Have students read their pieces aloud and have classmates guess what objects they have written as.

Writing Myths and Fables

Many myths were created to explain situations for which early people had no other explanation. Even though we now have scientific explanations for many natural occurrences, students can write their own stories to explain such things as why the sky is blue, why animals have fur, or why it snows.

Fables are stories with a moral. Read or tell students about one of Aesop's fables. Then brainstorm a list of "morals": "Two heads are better than one." "Always make two trips when one will almost do." "Don't look a gift horse in the mouth." Students choose one and write a fable.

"Parentisms"

Mothers and fathers through the ages have passed on wisdom by repeating what their parents said to them: "Don't talk with your mouth full." "You'll catch more flies with honey than with vinegar." "Children should be seen and not heard." Have students think about expressions their parents use and brainstorm a list of "parentisms." They may be surprised to discover how much all of their parents have in common.

Classified Ad Character Sketch

Collect some personal classified ads or write some of your own. Give one to students to read and then imagine what the person is like who wrote the ad. Have them write a piece telling about this person. Example of an ad: "Teenager wants job wallpapering or painting. Experienced. Rates reasonable. Call 729-8284 after 5 P.M." (How old is he/she? What experience does he/she have? Why does he/she need the money? Etc.)

"I Used To Think, but Now I Know"

Have students write down childhood beliefs that are laughable now. "I used to think that my father could make the light turn green by touching the dashboard." "I used to think 'Silent Night' had somthing to do with God's vegetables because of the words, 'deep in heavenly peas.'"

Shaped Verse

Concrete poems are visual, quick to write and fun to do. Have students look at the examples below and then write some of their own.

Students can also write poems which are shaped to fit the subject. The words in a poem about a tree would be written on the page to look like a tree for example.

Figure 8

EXAMPLES OF CONCRETE POEMS

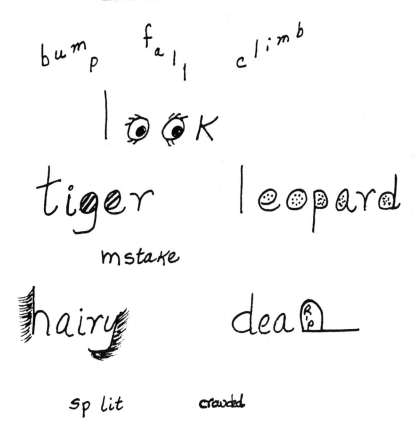

Haiku and Tanka

The structure of these poems is simple. Students count syllables for these three- or five-line poems. The Japanese poems by tradition also contain some reference either explicit or implicit to a season, but students don't need to be bound by this requirement.

Haiku - three lines: 5 syllables in the first line
                      7 syllables in the second line
                      5 syllables in the last line

After silver rains
Cool breezes bring to me the
Sweet scent of lilacs.

Tanka - five lines: 5 syllables in the first line
                      7 syllables in the second line
                      5 syllables in the third line
                      7 syllables in the fourth line
                      7 syllables in the last line

The sun hides, the wind
Dies, and dark clouds fill the sky.
The storm god wakes up,
Softly groans, grumbles, then cracks,
And flashes an evil grin.

Diamond-Shaped Poem (Diamanté)

In this form students begin with a noun and write a diamond-shaped poem which ends up being the opposite of the word they began with.

Line 1: Noun
Line 2: Two adjectives describing the noun
Line 3: Three participles (-ed, -ing)
Line 4: Four words, phrase about the noun in line one
Line 5: Three participles that begin to show a change in the subject
Line 6: Two adjectives which continue the change
Line 7: Noun, the opposite of the noun in line one

Friends
Close, happy
Laughing, playing, hugging
Someone who keeps secrets
Misunderstanding, shouting, crying
Angry, hurt
Enemies

Five-Line Poem (Cinquain)

Line 1: Noun (title of poem)
Line 2: Two adjectives describing noun
Line 3: Three verb forms used as adjectives
Line 4: Short phrase about noun
Line 5: A synonym for the noun in line one

Cats

Soft, cuddly
Purring, playing, sleeping
Fur friends to hold
Kittens

SOCIAL STUDIES

Create a Country

Have students make up a country. Name it, describe its natural features, resources, type of government, and so on. They may wish to make maps of their countries and write the information up as it would appear in an almanac. (You can use an actual entry as a model.) This activity can be done by students as individuals, in pairs, or in small groups. Share the finished products with the whole class.

Imaginary Island

Have students make maps of imaginary islands and label all the land features. This is a good way to have them review terms they have been learning in geography.

What Would Happen If...?

Have students imagine what would have been the result if some historical event had happened another way: If the South had won the Civil War, if John F. Kennedy had not been assassinated, if Hitler had not been stopped, etc.

News Stories

Have students write historical occurrences as if they were current news stories. Use articles from the newspaper or newsmagazines as models and remind them of the 5 W's in news stories: who, what, where, when, and why.

Milestones

A good semester- or year-end review exercise for students is having them make a list of what they consider milestones in the period of history they have been studying. Have students compare their lists when they finish and discuss why they chose the milestones they did. (If they do this activity without books, it will be more meaningful since they will have to think rather than merely copy what the textbook authors considered important.)

SCIENCE

Greatest Scientific Development

Have students select what they consider to be the greatest scientific development to date and why. Share responses and discuss.

Thinking About the Future

Have students write about what they think will happen in the future as the result of some recent scientific breakthrough. Share and discuss.

What We Need To Find Out

Have students think and write about what scientific discoveries are most needed now and why. Share and discuss.

Classification Activities

To help students understand how and why categories are created to organize information (such as in the classifications for plant and animal species), give them a box with a number of different items selected at random (paper clip, rubber bands, anything you can find). Ask them to divide the items into smaller groups on the basis of some criteria they select and then into still smaller groups based on other criteria. Then have them write down their classifications and criteria to share with classmates.

Another way to use some criteria to make decisions is to play a guessing game. One person thinks of an object in sight and gives a clue, for example, "It is round." Students write down all the round objects in sight. Then another criteria is mentioned: "It is blue." Students eliminate all items which are not blue, and so on.

Anti-Litter Campaign

Concern for the environment must start at home. Have students design an anti-litter campaign for their school or community.

ANY SUBJECT

Contest Entry

In twenty-five words or less tell why people should study "X." Have students select the best response.

Crossword Puzzle

Have students make up a crossword puzzle using names and terms from the subject they are studying. Give the puzzles to classmates to solve.

Make A Test

Have students make up a test on the material they are studying along with an answer key. If there's time, have them swap tests and take each other's.

Interview Questions

Have students select an expert in the field they are studying or a famous historical or literary character and then make up questions they would ask the person if they had a chance to interview him/her in person. If they choose historical or literary figures, they might also wish to role play the interviews.

Writing for Children

If you can explain something in your own words, then you truly understand it. Ask students to rewrite the information in a chapter from their textbook so that a child in the third or fourth grade would understand the main points.

Chapter Summary

Ask students to summarize the chapter in their text in fifty words or less. Compare summaries to see who did the best job of including all the main points in a clear and organized manner.

Figure 9

AN EXAMPLE OF A CONCEPT MAP BASED ON A SECTION IN A U.S. HISTORY TEXTBOOK.

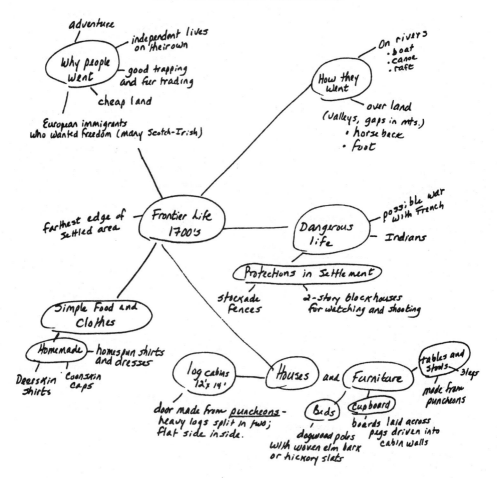

"How Did People Live in the Frontier Region?"
This Is America's Story, pp. 101-106. (Houghton Mifflin, 1981)

Concept Map

Have students "outline" the information in a chapter from their text-book in a diagram rather than a linear outline. The topic of the chapter appears in the center of the page in a circle; main points appear else-where on the page in circles connected by lines to the chapter topic. Minor points are written in and similarly connected by lines to the topic with which they connect. Have students share and discuss finished maps. See the sample concept map.

Chapter Nine

QUIZZES, WORD GAMES, AND OTHER CHALLENGES

PUT YOUR THIMKING [*sic*] CAP ON!

1. If you went to bed at 8 at night and set the alarm (on a non-digital clock) to get up at 9 in the morning, how many hours of sleep would you get?
2. Do they have a Fourth of July in England?
3. Why can't a person living in Durham, North Carolina, be buried west of the Mississippi?
4. How many birthdays does the average person have?
5. If you had only one match and you entered a room in which you found a kerosene lamp, an oil burner, and a wood-burning stove, which would you light first?
6. Some months have 30 days, some 31; how many have 28 days?
7. If a doctor gave you three pills and told you to take one every half hour, how long would they last?
8. A man builds a house with four sides to it, it's rectangular in shape, and each side has a southern exposure. A bear comes walking by. What color is the bear?
9. What four words appear on every United States coin?
10. How far can a dog run into a ten-mile round woods?
11. What is the minimum number of baseball players on the field during any part of an inning? How many outs are there in an inning?
12. I have two United States coins in my hand which total 55 cents. One is not a nickel. What are the coins?
13. A farmer had 17 sheep. All but nine died. How many did he have left?

14. Two men playing checkers played five games, and each man won the same number of games. How can you figure this?
15. If two is company and three is a crowd, what are four and five?
16. Take two apples from three apples and what do you have?
17. An archeologist claimed that he found some gold coins dated 40 B.C. Was he telling the truth?
18. A woman gives a beggar 50 cents. The woman is the beggar's sister, but the beggar is not the woman's brother. Why?
19. How many animals of each species did Moses take aboard the Ark with him?
20. Is it legal in Arkansas for a man to marry his widow's sister?

Answers

1. One hour
2. Yes
3. A living person can't be buried.
4. One birth day or one birthday a year
5. The match
6. All of them
7. One hour
8. White (He's at the South Pole.)
9. In God We Trust or United States of America
10. Five miles (then he's on the way out)
11. Zero if the teams are changing in the middle of an inning; six
12. A fifty-cent piece and a nickel (One is not a nickel, but the other is!)
13. Nine
14. They weren't playing each other.
15. Nine
16. Two apples
17. No. B.C. wasn't used until after A.D. began.
18. Her sister; the beggar is a woman.
19. None, Noah, not Moses, went on the Ark.
20. No. A man who has a widow would be dead.

CAN YOU FOLLOW DIRECTIONS?

If students have not done this exercise before, it is a very effective way of teaching them to read and follow directions. Make copies and give one to each student.

1. Read everything before doing anything.

2. Put your name in the upper right hand corner of this page.
3. Circle the word **name** in sentence two.
4. Draw five small squares in the upper left hand corner of the page.
5. Put an "X" in each square.
6. Put a circle around each square.
7. Sign your name under the title.
8. After the title write, "Yes, Yes, Yes."
9. Put a circle around each word in sentence seven.
10. Put an "X" in the lower left hand corner of this paper.
11. Draw a triangle around the "X" you just made.
12. On the reverse side of this paper, multiply 7 x 98.
13. Draw a triangle around the word **page** in sentence four.
14. Call out your first name when you get to this point in the test.
15. If you think you have followed directions to this point in the test, call out, "I have!"
16. On the reverse side of this paper, add 8950 and 9850.
17. Put a circle around your answer. Now put a square around the circle.
18. Count out loud in your normal speaking voice backwards from ten to one.
19. Now that you have finished reading carefully, do only sentences one and two.

CAN YOU SPOT THE SENTENCES AMONG THESE OLD SONG TITLES?

Read each title. If the title is a complete sentence, write "yes" beside each number. If not, write "no."
1. "You and the Night and the Music"
2. "Button Up Your Overcoat"
3. "Brother, Can You Spare a Dime?"
4. "Dream a Little Dream of Me"
5. "The Blue-Tail Fly"
6. "I Could Have Danced All Night"
7. "Three O'Clock in the Morning"
8. "Home, Sweet Home"
9. "Get Me to the Church on Time"
10. "Look for the Silver Lining"
11. "Smoke Gets in Your Eyes"

12. "Deep in the Heart of Texas"
13. "On Behalf of the Visiting Firemen"
14. "On the Sunny Side of the Street"
15. "Don't Fence Me In"
16. "Wake Up, Jacob"
17. "On Top of Old Smoky"
18. "Carry Me Back to Old Virginny"
19. "Do They Think of Me at Home?"
20. "Can't You Dance the Polka?"
21. "I Never Will Marry"
22. "In the Good Old Summertime"
23. "Just Before the Battle, Mother"
24. "Swinging on a Star"
25. "California, Here I Come"
26. "The Wearing of the Green"
27. "Younger than Springtime"
28. "Listen to the Mockingbird"

Answers

1. No
2. Yes
3. Yes
4. Yes
5. No
6. Yes
7. No
8. No
9. Yes
10. Yes
11. Yes
12. No
13. No
14. No
15. Yes
16. Yes
17. No
18. Yes
19. Yes
20. Yes
21. Yes

22. No
23. No
24. No
25. Yes
26. No
27. No
28. Yes

"I'M DYING, HE CROAKED.

"She said" and "he said" aren't the only ways to write a speech tag. As you can see from the title, what makes these quotations fun is that the speech tag is related in meaning to what the person said. Here are some other samples. Read them and then write some "punny" quotations and speech tags of your own.

"We missed the whale," she blubbered.

"Fasten your pants," he snapped.

"These jeans are too tight," she panted.

"Cut those fingernails," she snipped.

"I ate the last candy bar," he snickered.

"I can't find the fish," he floundered.

"I like birds," he chirped.

SNIGLETS

Rich Hall in his *Sniglets* books lists words that aren't in any dictionary but should be. Read the samples below. Then invent some words of your own that should be added to the dictionary. Include the part of speech and a definition for each.

ACCORDIONATED, adj. Being able to drive and refold a road map at the same time.

DETERRENCY, n. Ruined currency found in pants pockets after laundering.

GLACKETT, n. The noisy ball inside a spray paint can.

BOVILEXIA, n. Uncontrollable urge to lean out the car window and yell, "Moo!" every time you pass a cow.

ROVALERT, n. System whereby one dog can quickly establish an entire neighborhood network of barking.

"CONJUGATING IRREGULAR VERBS"

Bertrand Russell, the British philospher and mathematician, interested his BBC radio listeners years ago in "conjugating irregular verbs." As you can see, these "irregular verbs" aren't really verbs at all but adjectives and nouns. They are written, however, in the manner in which verbs are conjugated. Notice that although all three statements have the same general meaning, the connotation for each moves progressively from positive to neutral to negative. Look at the examples below and then try writing some of your own.

I am firm. You are obstinate. He is a pig-headed fool.

I am slender. You are thin. He is skinny as a rail.

I daydream. You are an escapist. He needs to see a psychiatrist.

BRAINSTORMING

Brainstorming is a way of generating lots of ideas. The focus is on quantity, not quality. The point is to come up with as many ideas as possible without stopping to evaluate them. Brainstorming helps develop creativity, and the results can later be used in problem solving.

These brainstorming exercises can be done by students as individuals, in pairs or triads, or in small groups. You can make up other items to use instead of or in addition to the ones listed below. You may wish to set a time limit and make the exercise a contest.

Think of as many uses as you can for the following. Imagine that you have only one or as many of the same item as you wish. Don't stop to evaluate your ideas. The object is to come up with as many ways as you can to use the objects. Silly ideas are okay. The more ideas you get, the better your ideas are likely to be.

How many ways can you use A BRICK?

How many ways can you use A TOOTHPICK?

How many ways can you use A ONE FOOT SQUARE SHEET OF ALUMINUM FOIL?

How many ways can you use A STICK OF GUM?

PROBLEM SOLVING EXERCISES

Students can be asked to brainstorm solutions to the problems below, and evaluate them, and then expand their better ideas. You may wish to develop other problems on which they can work in addition to the ones given here.

Be creative. How many ways can you think of that might work to solve the following problems. After you've brainstormed a number of possibilities, choose your best one and write about it in a paragraph or two to share with your classmates.

HOW CAN YOU GET A DOG AND CAT TO STOP FIGHTING?
HOW CAN YOU FIX A WALK SO THAT IT DOESN'T NEED TO BE SHOVELED AFTER IT SNOWS?
WHAT CAN A MOTHER DO TO KEEP TABS ON A TODDLER WITHOUT WATCHING HIM/HER EVERY MINUTE?

INVENTIONS

Inventions are another way students can exercise their creative muscles. Have them work alone, in pairs, or in small groups to come with inventions for the following (or develop some other ideas of your own on which they can work).

A HOUSE FOR A CAT, DOG, OR SQUIRREL
A SELF-WATERING PLANT POT
A BED MADE ONLY FROM NATURAL MATERIALS WHICH COULD BE FOUND IN A FOREST OR FIELD
A NEW PRODUCT OF YOUR CHOICE--COSMETIC ITEMS ARE BIG SELLERS!

INVENTIONS FOLLOW-UP

After students have invented their new products, have them develop an advertising campaign for them. They can design at least one magazine or newspaper ad, one television or radio commercial, and/or a brochure describing the product. They might also include special promotional gimmicks or activities they would use, such as special introductory offers, store displays, direct mailing materials, discount coupons, etc. Have them share their results with the rest of the class. [Note: This activity can be limited to one period or expanded for a couple of days.]

SMALL GROUP CREATIVE CRAFTS

To give students the opportunity to improve their ability to work with others in a small group and to develop their creativity, collect a variety of unrelated materials out of which something could be constructed: string, clay, toothpicks, crumpled aluminum foil, baking cups, styrofoam packing chips, etc. Along with the raw materials, give each group scissors, glue or tape, and markers. Set a time limit and tell students that each group must create something with the materials available. When the time is up, the groups can present their "creations" to the class. A prize might be given for the most original idea. Because this exercise is a good training exercise for small group process, also have students discuss **how** their groups worked: how they got organized, how long it took, who contributed, who failed to do their fair share, and so forth. Groups which function more smoothly usually, but not always, have the better products.

METAPHORICAL CATEGORIES

This game, which is similiar to "Twenty Questions," will help students develop new ways of thinking about people. One student chooses a well-known living, fictional, or historical person. He or she then tells the class, "I am thinking of a male rock star." The other students then ask questions which reveal the essence of the person, not factual information about him: What food is he most like? What animal would you associate with him? What kind of car does he remind you of? What kind of weather seems most like his personality? What season (color/time of day/etc.) is he most like? The person who guesses correctly then takes the next turn thinking of someone and answering questions from classmates. Score like "Twenty Questions" or by counting the number of questions that are asked before someone guesses correctly--lowest score wins--with additional points to the person who guesses correctly.

OPEN YOUR EYES

The quiz below is a general one. If you frequently substitute in the same school, make up an observation quiz based on specifics in that school. (What color are the walls in the main office? What shape are the tables in the cafeteria? etc.)

1. Will the moon tomorrow night be fuller or less full when it appears tonight as a crescent moon shaped like a C?
2. In what direction do revolving doors turn?
3. What two letters do NOT appear on a telephone dial?
4. Name the five colors on a Campbell's soup label.
5. When you walk, do your arms swing with or against the rhythm of your legs?
6. Is the green on most traffic lights on the top or bottom?
7. In what direction do pieces travel around a Monopoly board, clockwise or counterclockwise?
8. What word appears in the center of the back of a one dollar bill?
9. Is the uppermost stripe on the American flag red or white?
10. How many matches are there in a standard pack of matches?
11. In the painting, "American Gothic" by Grant Wood, is the man to the viewer's left or right?
12. In what hand does the Statue of Liberty hold her torch?
13. How many channels are on a standard VHF television dial?
14. Which side of a woman's blouse has the buttonholes on it from her view wearing the blouse--right or left?
15. How many sides does a standard pencil have?

Answers

1. Waning or less full. The full moon follows a D-shaped moon.
2. Counterclockwise.
3. Q and Z.
4. Black, white, gold, red, and yellow.
5. Against.
6. On the bottom.
7. Clockwise.
8. The word ONE.
9. Red.
10. Twenty.
11. Right.
12. Right.
13. Twelve (There's no channel 1).
14. Right.
15. Six.

BRAINSTORMING CLICHÉS

Here are some examples of comparisons which have become common expressions. How many more can you think of?

He was as clever as a fox.

Her mind was like a steel trap.

He came out smelling like a rose.

She was as grouchy as a bear.

He was as fat as a pig.

She was as wise as an owl.

She avoided him like the plague.

REWRITING CLICHÉS

Clichés are no longer fresh and original because everyone uses them. Rewrite some of the clichés you brainstormed in the previous exercise so that they are new and different.

Examples: She was as grouchy as a bear. Rewritten: She was as grouchy as an overworked waitress in a crowded restaurant.

He was as clever as a fox. Rewritten: He was as clever as a computer.

"FORMULAS" TO FIGURE OUT

Richard Lederer, a teacher at St. Paul's School in Concord, New Hampshire, made up this unusual quiz to challenge readers of his popular column on language in the *Maine Sunday Telegram*.

These "formulas" are really only initials for basic facts or popular sayings. How many can you decipher?

Examples: 7 D = 1 W Seven days equal one week.

26 L in the A = 26 letters in the alphabet

1. 3 F = 1 Y
2. A + E + I + O + U = V
3. 50 S = USA
4. S + S + M + T + W + T + F = D of the W
5. M + NH + V + M + RI + C = NE
6. S + H of R = USC
7. "A P S = A P E"
8. 24 H = 1 D

9. N + P + V + A + A + P + C + I = the P O S
10. M + M + L + J = 4 G
11. 4 K + 4 Q + 4 J = the FC
12. 8 P or 4 Q = 1 G
13. 12 M = 1 Y
14. 100 Y = 1 FBF
15. 18H = a GC
16. "1 B in the H = 2 in the B"
17. D + H + G + S + B + S + D = the 7D
18. 54C in a D (with J)
19. 1000 C = 1 M
20. 26 M + 385 Y = 1 M
21. "1 S in T S 9"
22. 60 M = 1 H
23. 32 D F = the T at which W F
24. 64 S on a CB
25. HH = MH at 12 = N or M
26. A + E were in the G of E
27. C + 6 D = NYE
28. "R = R = R"
29. AL + JG + WM + JFK = A P
30. 26 A in the C
31. 13 S + 50 S on the AF
32. 360 D = the C of C
33. the N + the P + the SM = C S
34. I B E except A C
35. "N P = N G"
36. 16 O = 1 P
37. P + B + K + R + K + Q = CP
38. 40 D = 40 N = the GF
39. a 4 LC = GL
40. B or G - F + M = O
41. 10 D = 1 C
42. "NN = GN"
43. 12 I = 1 F
44. 9 P = the SS
45. 5,280 F = 1 M
46. P + A + A = the 3 M
47. "N = the M of I"

48. 3 BM (SHTR)
49. B + R + Y = the PC
50. 90 D = a RA

Answers

1. 3 feet = 1 yard
2. a, e, i, o, and u = vowels
3. 50 states in the USA
4. Saturday, Sunday, Monday, Tuesday, Wednesday, Thursday, and Friday = the days of the week
5. Maine, New Hampshire, Vermont, Massachusetts, Rhode Island, and Connecticut make up New England.
6. The Senate and the House of representatives make up the US Congress.
7. "A penny saved is a penny earned."
8. 24 hours in a day
9. noun, pronoun, verb, adjective, adverb, prepostion, conjunction, and interjection are the parts of speech.
10. Matthew, Mark, Luke, and John are the four gospels.
11. 4 kings, 4 queens, and 4 jacks are the face cards.
12. 8 pints or 4 quarts equal a gallon.
13. 12 months equal one year.
14. 100 yards make a football field.
15. 18 holes in a golf course
16. "A bird in the hand is worth two in the bush."
17. Doc, Happy, Grumpy, Sneezy, Bashful, Sleepy, and Dopey are the 7 Dwarfs.
18. 54 cards in a deck (with jokers)
19. 1,000 centuries equal a millennium.
20. 26 miles and 385 yards equal a marathon.
21. "A stitch in time saves nine."
22. 60 minutes equal one hour.
23. 32 degrees Fahrenheit is the temperature at which water freezes.
24. 64 squares on a chess or checker board.
25. Hour hand and minute hand at 12 is noon or midnight.
26. Adam and Eve were in the Garden of Eden
27. Christmas plus 6 days is New Year's Eve.
28. "A rose is a rose is a rose."
29. Abraham Lincoln, James Garfield, William McKinley, and John F. Kennedy were assassinated presidents.

30. 26 amendments in the Constitution
31. 13 stripes and 50 stars are on the American flag.
32. 360 degrees in the circumference of a circle
33. The Nina, the Pinta, and the Santa Maria were Columbus's ships.
34. i before e except after c
35. "No pain, no gain."
36. 16 ounces make a pound.
37. Pawn, bishop, knight, rook, king, and queen are chess pieces.
38. 40 days and 40 nights were the Great Flood.
39. A four-leaf clover is good luck.
40. A boy or girl without a father and mother is an orphan.
41. 10 decades in a century
42. "No news is good news."
43. 12 inches is a foot.
44. 9 planets in the solar system
45. 5,280 feet make a mile.
46. Porthos, Aramis and Athos are the Three Musketeers.
47. "Necessity is the mother of invention."
48. 3 blind mice (see how they run)
49. Blue, red, and yellow are the primary colors.
50. 90 degrees make a right angle.

Challenge

Can you make up any new "formulas" with which to stump your class-mates?

LICENSE PLATE SLOGANS

Match the slogans with the states.

1. Arizona	a.	Live Free or Die
2. Arkansas	b.	The First State
3. Connecticut	c.	Vacationland
4. Delaware	d.	Constitution State
5. Louisiana	e.	America's Dairyland
6. Maine	f.	Wild Wonderful
7. Minnesota	g.	Green Mountain
8. New Hampshire	h.	Volunteer State
9. New Mexico	i.	Grand Canyon State
10. Pennsylvania	j.	Ocean State

11. Rhode Island
12. Tennessee
13. Vermont
14. West Virginia
15. Wisconsin

k. Land of Opportunity
l. You've Got a Friend in ...
m. Land of Enchantment
n. Sportsman's Paradise
o. 10,000 Lakes

Answers

1. i
2. k
3. d
4. b
5. n
6. c
7. o
8. a
9. m
10. l
11. j
12. h
13. g
14. f
15. e

TRIVIA, CURRENT EVENTS, OR CULTURAL LITERACY QUIZZES

Make up your own list of trivia or general knowledge questions and take them with you when you substitute. There are many trivia books available if you need help coming up with good questions. E.D. Hirsch's bestseller **Cultural Literacy** is a good source for general knowledge questions.

Whenever you find yourself with a few minutes in class and nothing to do, pull out your question list and challenge the students. This activity can be expanded to fill the time available. Students can write individual answers to the questions or you can set up a competition among rows. Another option is to ask students to construct their own trivia or general knowledge questions and challenge their classmates to a duel of minds.

If you are substituting for a social studies teacher, make your quiz questions about events and people currently in the news.

SPELLING AND OTHER BEES

The old standby, the spelling bee, is another good activity to keep students busy and interested when the teacher has left no plans. Instead of spelling words, you can give students vocabulary words to define or usage exercises to complete (The book [was were] on the table). If you're substituting in a subject area other than English/language arts, adapt the bee to the subject by choosing words to spell that come from the particular subject or by asking review questions from the textbook. You can set up a math bee on the multiplication tables or computational problems students can do in their heads.

DICTIONARY OR ENCYCLOPEDIA RACE

Make up a list of words to locate in the dictionary or facts to find in an encyclopedia (or textbook). Give each student a copy of them face down. When you say go, they turn their sheets over and begin their searches, noting the page and other information you requested on their papers. The first person (or team) which finishes with the correct answers wins. If you have only a few minutes to fill, give the information orally with the students looking for only one item each time. This way everyone will be "finished" whenever the bell rings.

ABSTRACT IDEAS EXERCISE

This exercise will show students how much and how little abstract words mean. First brainstorm a long list of abstract nouns and write them on the board: fear, power, freedom, love, joy, pain, etc. Number each abstract noun listed. Then write the frames below on the board or have them ready on a handout.

1. WHEN _____ BECOMES _____, THEN IS _____ .
2. _____ WITHOUT _____ IS _____ .
3. _____ ENDS WHEN _____ BEGINS.
4. NOT _____ NOR _____, BUT _____ AND _____ .
5. THIS IS AN AGE OF _____ AND _____ .
6. _____ AND _____
7. THE _____ OF _____

Have students call out the numbers on the board at random. Going in order through the blanks in the frames, fill in whatever abstract noun comes up. (Example: When fear becomes power, then is freedom.) Students will be amazed at how these words fit in and make some sense. Of course, the reason they do is that abstract words have general rather than specific meanings. As you continue with this process a few times, have students jot down the phrases that seem especially appealing to them.

If you have enough time, have students choose one of the phrases they wrote down and pretend it is the title of a new book. Then ask them to write a "jacket blurb" or review for the book and later read their pieces aloud.

INFERENCES

People often get themselves into trouble because they draw the wrong conclusions from a given set of circumstances. Have students respond to the situations below. Then share "Further Information" with them and discuss what they wrote.

HOW WOULD YOU EXPLAIN EACH OF THE FOLLOWING SITUATIONS?

1. A broken vase is lying on the floor. The little girl in the room has a very worried look on her face.
2. Mr. Smith drives to work every morning at 7:30 A.M. His wife walks along the same street to her job at 7:35 A.M.
3. A boy looks very unhappy as he sits outside the door to the principal's office. A teacher with an angry look on her face stands nearby.
4. The Jones family has lived in their house for two years. Yet they have no furniture in either the formal dining room or living room.
5. School starts at 8 A.M. At 8:30 A.M. Mr. Brown, who knows Tom is a student, sees him downtown.
6. Mary comes to class for the third day in a row and doesn't have her homework done.
7. Mr. Saunders goes to Europe about four times every year.
8. Sally, who is fourteen, didn't get home Saturday night until 2 A.M.

Further Information

1. The little girl just came into the room and found the broken vase. She knows her mother will be upset and fears that her dog is responsible.

2. Mrs. Smith is dieting and wants the exercise she gets from walking to work.
3. The little boy is waiting for his mother to pick him up for a doctor's appointment. The teacher is waiting to talk with the principal about a personal matter.
4. The Jones family had only a limited amount of money to spend. They decided to put a swimming pool in the backyard first and buy furniture for those rooms later. They spend most of their time in a family room which is comfortably and tastefully furnished.
5. Tom is downtown doing an errand for the teacher.
6. Mary has an eye problem. The doctor told her not to do any reading or writing for a week.
7. Mr. Saunders works for a European company and must go to the corporate headquarters for meetings.
8. Sally was babysitting for a neighbor.

Chapter Ten

GENERAL PUBLICATIONS AS RESOURCES

THE ACTIVITIES in this chapter all depend upon having material from newspapers, television viewing guides, magazines, or travel brochures and schedules. If you don't know whether you will have access to class sets of newspapers or magazines to use, read through the activities described and make photocopied handouts of the parts of these publications that you'll need for activities you want to do. For most of the activities it isn't necessary for students to have copies of the same issue so you could bring in back issues of your own magazines and newspapers.

THINGS TO DO WITH NEWSPAPERS

Elementary Activities

Exploring the Newspaper

*What can you find in the newspaper?. Where is it located? (weather, TV listings, sports, local news, etc.)
*How many ways can a person get his/her name in the paper? (important people--politicians, TV stars, sports heroes, criminals, people who die, etc.)
*What can you buy? List items and where they are sold. (Tires-department store, auto store; groceries-supermarket; etc.)
*How many careers can you find mentioned? (Look first everywhere in the paper except the classified ads; then check the ads.)

Looking at the Comics

1. Find a comic character who is not human.
2. Find one who makes mistakes.
3. Find one who's a child.
4. Find a comic with only one frame.
5. Find a comic kids would prefer.
6. Find one adults would like.
7. Tell what your favorite comic is and why.

All About Me

1. Find a car you'd like to own.
2. Find a job you'd like to try.
3. Find a movie you'd like to see.
4. Find something you'd like to buy
5. And something you'd like to eat.
6. Find your favorite sports team
7. And a person you'd like to meet.
8. Find your horoscope for the day.

News Stories--the 5 W's

Have students read stories in the paper and find the 5 W's: Who, What, When, Where, and Why. Then have them write their own. Example:

Who: Susie Samuels, age 8

What: Lost her lunch money

When: Yesterday

Where: On the way to school

Why: Because she wore her oldest jeans even after her mother told her not to. The money fell out of a big hole in her pocket.

Primary Math

*Money: Look at the food store ads. Mark the items costing more than $1 with one color. Use another color to mark the items costing less than $1.

*Shopping: Give students a certain amount of money to spend. Have them cut or mark the items they would buy with it.

*Comparisons: Using ads or photos, circle the biggest items in one color; the smallest in another.

*Counting: Have students count various objects, letters, words, etc.

*Numerals: Have students find and cut out various examples of numerals. They can then paste these on a sheet of paper. (You might ask for one example of the numeral 1, two examples of 2, and so forth.)

*Shapes: Have students locate and color in various shapes: triangles, squares, circles, etc. Or cut them out and paste them on a sheet of paper.

Primary Social Studies

*Community Helpers: Find examples of pictures and articles of people who can help others in various ways.

*Shopping for the Family: Find examples of all the things a family probably needs to have. (You can discuss here the difference between **needing** and **wanting**.)

*Shelter: Find examples of different types of shelters (houses, motels, apartments, etc.) Students can cut these out and make a house-shaped class collage.

*Weather: Read the weather forecasts from some recent issues and see if they were right. Or read tomorrow's forecast and follow up to see if it was right.

*Categories: Find examples of different kinds of transportation or information about or items concerned with safety, accidents, etc.

Primary Language Arts

*Find examples of the letters of the alphabet and words that begin with each. Make an alphabet collage or scrapbook.

*Alphabet Monster: Cut out all kinds of things beginning with A and glue to backing paper in the shape of an "A" monster. Do the same for B, C, etc.

*Word Search: Have students look for certain kinds of words--rhyming, with certain beginning consonants, a certain number of syllables, etc,-- or words they don't know the meanings of but would like to.

Elementary Math

*Math Concepts: Find words that show SIZE (biggest, smallest), LOCATION (high, low), TIME (two weeks, ten-year), QUANTITY (all, none, many, fewer), VALUE (100% wool, heavyweight), MONEY ($3.98 is almost $4.00; 10% off is how much?), and RELATIONSHIP (equal to, up 13% from last year).

*Housing Costs: Find the comparable houses in the classified ads and see how the prices compare for each type and how they vary by location.

*Salaries/Wages: Check the classified ads to find typical wages or salaries for various occupations. Which require special training or more education?

*Shopping: Compare prices for food or other items at different stores.

Elementary Social Studies

*Taxes: Find out the different types of taxes we pay.

*Time Capsule: Cut out stories, articles, ads, etc. that you would include in a time capsule.

*Conservation: Cut out articles and pictures about conservation activities.

*Respecting Rules: Find stories about people who broke the rules. What happened (or will happen) to them?

*Transportation: List types of transportation and current problems.

*Famous Quotes: Find examples of quotes from famous people. Which are important. Why?

*History Repeats: Find examples of current events that seem to repeat past events.

Elementary Language Arts

*Applying for a Job: Find a job opening in the classified ads. Write a letter telling why you would be a good person for the job.

*Write your own classified ad for an item you'd like to buy or sell.

*Answer one of the ads in the pets-for-sale column telling why you'd be a good person to adopt that pet.

*Read the advice column. Then write your own letter asking for advice (You can make up a problem or use a real one). Swap letters with classmates and write replies to each other. Another possibility; write your own response to one of the letters that appears in the column. [Or the teacher can read one of these letters aloud to the class, have the students write replies, and then compare theirs with the advice columnist's.]

*Read a feature article. Then try writing one of your own about a subject you know well in your own school.

*Write some humorous classified ads for made-up products.

*Design a display ad selling people on your class or your school.

*Write a "Help Wanted" ad for the ideal teacher (perhaps the one you'd like to have next year) or the perfect student.

Elementary Science

*Weather: Write an article about a current weather problem (too little rain, too much snow, etc.) and how people are dealing with it.

*Pollution: Research articles on pollution problems and write an article explaining one and how it might be solved.

*Make your own weather calendar, complete with symbols, and track the weather for a week.

*Scientific Progress in Advertising: Find examples of ads which include new developments/breakthroughs/improvements.

Elementary Health

*Stay Healthy: Find examples of articles or ads that tell how to stay healhy.

*Menu Planning: Using the grocery ads, plan a nutritious menu for a family of four for a day or a week.

*Favorite Meal: Find the items you would buy for your favorite meal and list the prices of each.

*Disease: Read articles on a disease. Write a report explaining the disease and how it might be prevented.

Secondary Activities

Secondary Math

*Commissions: Using 13 percent as the amount you would earn for a commission, figure out what you would be paid for selling various types of autos and trucks advertised.

*Finance Charges: Figure out what the finance charges would amount to on a car or house loan using figures in the ads and selecting a car and house you'd like to own.

*Savings Interest: Assume you have $1000 to put in the bank. Check the bank ads to find the best rate. How much would your money earn in a year?

*Money Conversion: Using the section which lists the current foreign exchange rates, convert $500 in American money to the currencies of several other countries.

*Measuring: Figure out how much carpet would cost for your classroom based on prices listed in an ad. (You'll have to measure your classroom.)

*Budgeting: Estimate how much it would cost you to live on your own for a month. Include food, shelter, and clothing priced as they appear in the ads.

Secondary Social Studies

*Employment: Analyze the employment opportunities in your area. What categories of jobs are available? What do they pay?

*U.S. Economy: Read all you can find in today's paper on the U.S. economy. Write a summary of your findings.

*What's New: How many of the products mentioned in the display ads were not available 20 years ago?

*Constitution: Find articles that relate to the U.S. Constitution and its amendments.

*Local Agencies: Make a list of all the local agencies that are mentioned in the paper. Find out what they do and whom they benefit.

*Taxes: Find articles that show how taxes are collected and how the money is used. Put this information into chart form.

*Labor Relations: Look for articles about labor-management relations. What's happening in your area?

*Leadership: Based on what you've been reading in the newspaper, make a list of the qualities people who are good leaders have. Who are the people in today's paper that have the qualities you listed?

Secondary Language Arts

*Write a limerick about a well-known person who appears in today's paper.

*Summarize a news story so that it could be read on a radio broadcast.

*Analyze an editorial cartoon. Try drawing one of your own.

*Typos Search: Newspapers are famous for the number of typographical errors they contain. See who in your class can find the most in the shortest time.

*Editorial Page: Read the page. Then write a letter to the editor giving your views on an editorial printed today or respond to one of the letters to the editor printed there.

*Write your own editorial, perhaps on a school issue.

*Facts vs. Opinions: Use the paper to find examples of each.

*Read through the whole issue of the paper. What do you think someone who's never been to your town would assume about your community from reading just this one issue? What kind of an impression does the newspaper create of your community?

*Write a feature article or news story about your school or community.

Secondary Science

*Energy Saving: Find examples in ads or articles of energy-saving concerns or products.
*Environment: Find examples which show a growing concern for protecting the environment.
*New Developments: Make a list of the new developments in science and technology as reflected in articles and advertising. What problems are developing or might develop as a result of this progress? What other advances do you predict will come in the future?

TV GUIDES AS RESOURCES

You can develop many one-period activities based on TV and radio. For some of these activities you'll need copies of **TV Guide** or the viewing guides that come in the newspaper or photocopies of material from them. Others can be done without any additional materials.

Have students complete either of the questionnaires below and then use their responses as the basis for a class discussion.

Radio and TV: Your Viewing and Listening Habits

1. How many of each of the following are available in your home? _____ TV sets _____ Radios
2. How much time do you listen to the radio on an average school day?
3. What station do you normally listen to?
4. What is its format?
5. Estimate the number of hours you usually watch TV on the following days:
   Sunday _____ Monday _____ Tuesday _____ Wednesday _____ Thursday _____ Friday _____ Saturday _____
   WEEKLY TOTAL: _____ HOURS
6. Is there a TV program(s) you never miss? _____ What?
7. What do you see as TV's greatest benefit?
8. In what ways do you think TV might be bad for society?
9. How would you feel if TV were completely eliminated?
10. What do you think would happen at home if your family were unable to watch TV for a week?

Questions about Television Series

1. What is your favorite TV series? Why?
2. Who is the most interesting character in the program? Why?
3. Who is the least interesting? Why?
4. How would you describe this series, e.g. sit-com, drama, adventure, police, soap, etc.?
5. Are the plots true-to-life? Explain.
6. Are the characters true-to-life or stereotyped? Explain.
7. In what ways could this show be made more educational without destroying its entertainment value? Give some examples.

Activities

*Analyze the prime-time schedule of the three major networks for one or two days. Make a chart showing the shows scheduled and the times. Why do you think the network executives decided to schedule the shows as they did?

*List the prime-time programs for a week. Categorize them according to the type of show each is (sit-com, drama, soap, etc.). Add up the number of hours you found for each category. What do you think your results say about Americans' viewing habits?

*Provide students with a random list of programs (real titles or made-up ones but enough to fill an evening's prime-time viewing on three stations). Have them schedule the programs for each station and explain their decisions.

*Using the TV schedule provided, write down the shows you think each of the following people will choose to view:

    an elderly man and woman living on a Social Security
    an eight-year-old girl
    a ten-year-old boy
    teenage girl
    teenage boy
    working class man who's divorced and living alone
    young mother whose executive husband works late or travels a lot
    your teacher
    the principal
    a widow who lives very comfortably by herself

*Have students read brief plot descriptions of unfamiliar movies or programs in a series with the identifying names omitted (so they can't recognize the show). Ask them to choose one and write a story based on the plot.

*Have students develop a new TV series and write the program description for it.

*Topic for discussion or writing: What would someone who knew nothing about the United States think the country was like from watching only _____ (Fill in one or two well-known TV shows.)

*Analyze several characters from some well-known series to determine whether or not they are stereotyped.

*Have students brainstorm a list of all the activities they could do at home rather than watch TV.

*Have students list all the stereotypes they see on TV.

ADVERTISING ACTIVITIES

Advertising--both print ads and television commercials--offer a rich source of material for activities for students. If you have a stack of old magazines, you can let students cut and tear these up. If not, photocopy or mount suitable ads for use in the classroom.

Advertising Analysis

The following are claims often used in ads. Use this material as a handout and have students use the information to analyze magazine and TV advertising.

The Unfinished Claim. The product is "better" or offers "more," but the ad never finishes the comparison. "Accent gives you More!" (NEW and IMPROVED are often used in this manner, too.)

The Weasel Word Claim. A weasel word is a modifier that makes what follows almost meaningless. The claims sound convincing, but when you look more carefully, you see that they are empty. Examples of weasel words: HELPS, VIRTUAL (VIRTUALLY), LIKE (when used to compare), ACTS, WORKS, CAN BE, UP TO, AS MUCH AS, REFRESHES, COMFORTS, FIGHTS, THE FEEL OF, THE LOOK OF, TASTES, FORTIFIED, ENRICHED, STRENGTHENED. "X leaves the dishes virtually spotless."

The "We're Different and Unique" Claim. There is nothing quite like the product advertised, but the difference may not be important. "Clean Detergent's pink power stands alone." (Does it matter if it's pink?)

The "Water Is Wet" Claim. The claim makes a statement that's true of every other similar product. "Glossy Shoe Polish polishes your shoes." The statement of fact is made to sound like a special benefit.

The "So What" Claim. This technique is similar to the "Water Is Wet" claim except it claims an advantage not shared by other similar products. "Strong enough for a man but made for a woman." So what?

The Vague Claim. The claim is simply not clear. The words are colorful, but the claim is meaningless. "Hair never looked so shiny."

The Endorsement or Testimonial. A celebrity or authority appears in the ad to give the advertiser's claims more stature whether or not there is any real connection between the person and the product. Famous people make big money doing these ads, and there's no guarantee they even use the products they speak for.

The Scientific or Statistical Claim. The advertising uses some sort of "scientific" proof, experiments, or impressive statistics to support their claims, "One out of every two doctors surveyed prescribes X," but you don't know how many doctors were surveyed or what kinds of doctors they might have been.

The "Compliment the Consumer" Claim. The ad flatters the consumer. Discriminating buyers choose X."

The Rhetorical Questions. A question is posed to which the viewer or listener is supposed to answer in a positive way. "Wouldn't you really rather have a Buick?"

The Honest Claim. Some ads actually make clear, true statements about the products.

Propaganda Devices

The propaganda devices as listed several years ago by the Institute of Propaganda Analysis can also be used to analyze and evaluate the claims of advertisers both in print and on televison. Some of these devices duplicate the claims listed above.

Name Calling. Applying some label that people generally dislike or fear to a person, organization, or an idea is a technique used to discredit rather than describe accurately. Words, such as RED, FACIST, ALIEN, etc. are often used in this way for political purposes. In advertising the label is often more subtle, "Why use that greasy kid stuff?"

Glittering Generality. A high-sounding word with a very clear meaning is used to get people to accept an idea or product without examining the facts. The use of FREEDOM, LOVE, and BEAUTY are examples.

Transfer. This device carries over the reputation or good feelings about something, someone, or some place to the product or idea being sold. A tropical island paradise, for example, is pictured as the background for a product that has little or no connection to the tropics.

Testimonial. Quoting some well-known person to lend an air of credibility or importance to what is being sold or advocated.

Plain Folks. An attempt to win confidence and favor by connecting the product or idea with the common people. (Motherhood and apple pie)

Card Stacking. Selecting and using the facts to give a false or misleading idea is a common trick. The idea may be to make the best case for a product or idea while making the situation look worse for the opposing side or simply choosing only those facts or figures which support the case and omitting mention of anything that doesn't support it. Figures don't lie, but liars can figure!

Band Wagon. This is often the device of choice for young people: "But, Ma, everybody else is..." Advertisers try to hook consumers the same way.

Your Feelings about Ads and Commercials

Have students respond to the following questions and use their responses as a basis for a class discussion.
1. What is your favorite magazine ad or TV commercial? Why?
2. What is the most honest ad or commercial you have seen?
3. What is the most persuasive ad or commercial you remember? Why was it effective?
4. What's the worst ad or commercial you have seen? Why?
5. What is the funniest or most entertaining ad or commercial you have seen? What made it special?

Ad Contest

An alternative to having a discussion based on the questionnaire above is having students use their responses in an ad contest. Have students give prizes to the following:
1. The World's Most Honest Ad
2. The Crooked Tongue Award--for skill in sneaky, misleading, and deceptive use of language in advertising
3. The At-Least-It's-Fun Award--to the most entertaining ad
4. The Foot-in-the-Door Award--to the most persuasive ad found

5. The Totally Tasteless Award
6. The World's Worst Advertisement

Other Advertising Activities

*Cut out ads aimed at particular audiences. Try to find ads directed to:
   homemakers
   blue-collar workers
   white-collar workers
   business executives
   teenagers
   people who are nearing or already at retirement age
*Make a list of TV commercials directed to particular audiences. Consider, for example, groups such as the following:
   children under ten
   young mothers/fathers
   singles
   urban dwellers
   suburban dwellers
   men
   women
   teenagers
   blue-collar workers
   executives
   retirees
*Identify print ads or TV commercials which appeal to the hidden needs of people to:
   look beautiful/handsome
   feel healthy and energetic
   be accepted
   find love and happiness
   be adventurous
   find emotional security
   acquire power
   be creative
*Compile a list of TV commercials you feel are in good taste and give reasons for your choice.
*Do the same with TV commercials you feel are in bad taste.
*Develop your own rating system for magazine and newspaper ads. Then cut out some ads and rate them. Consider the following criteria:

reasonable basis for claims made
effective use of language
appropriateness and appeal of design
respect for intelligence of audience
*Develop your own rating system for TV commercials. You can adapt the criteria listed above. Then use your system to rate some commercials.
*Write you own print ad or television commercial selling an invented product, your class, or your school to others.

TRAVEL BROCHURES AS TEXTBOOKS

You can collect travel brochures, airline or bus schedules, and maps and use these as the basis for several class activities. Check your library for the addresses of the national tourist offices for other countries and tourist bureaus in the various states to whom you can write for materials. Again, you can make up class sets of materials needed by photocopying handouts if you can't gather enough original material.

Here are several ways to use the travel information in class. You'll no doubt be able to come with others.
*Trip Planning: Using brochures which describe places of interest in an area or country, have students plan a schedule of sightseeing for several days or a week or a month-long tour. This can be a simple exercise just planning how the time would be spent or made more complex by including cost, comparison shopping to find the best travel bargains.
*Math Exercises: Using foreign exchange rate and clothing size conversion charts, have students find out how much their American money is worth and what sizes they would look for when shopping overseas. Students can use the exchange rate information to make a comparison price chart to carry with them while they shop so they would have an idea what the price of the foreign item is in American dollars. [The French Government Tourist Office, 610 Fifth Avenue, New York, NY 10020-2452 publishes a booklet called *The Parisian's Guide to Paris Shopping* which contain both clothing size conversion charts for men and women and lists of stores at which various items may be purchased.]
*Learning with Maps: Using maps of cities or countries, have students plan and mark routes for their daily sightseeing or overall travel.
*Reading Schedules: Using airline, bus, or train schedules, have students find out how long it takes to get from one place to another, etc. You

can make this a kind of scavenger hunt by asking a series of questions which lead students from one point in the schedule to another. The one who finishes first with the correct answers wins. *Airport Flight Guide,* updated four times a year lists all flights to and from the three New York area airports (Kennedy International, LaGuardia, and Newark International) is fun to use for this activity because the planes fly to exotic places. Students can be asked to figure out flight times when planes must cross several time zones, including the International Dateline. [Write Airport Flight Guide, One World Trade Center 65 N, New York, NY 10048.]

*Traveling at Home: All of these activities can be done using information only from the local area or home state. An additional project: write a travel brochure for your region or school.

APPENDIX

STATE DEPARTMENTS OF EDUCATION

ALABAMA
State Department of Education
Montgomery, AL 36130

ALASKA
Alaska Department of Education
P.O. Box F
Juneau, AK 99811

ARIZONA
Teacher Certification Unit
Arizona Department of Education
1535 West Jeferson
P.O. Box 25609
Phoenix, AZ 85002

ARKANSAS
State Department of Education
Building 4, Capitol Mall
Little Rock, AR 72201

CALIFORNIA
Commission of Teacher Credentialing
State Department of Public Instruction
721 Capitol Mall
Sacramento, CA 95814

COLORADO
State Department of Education
201 East Colfax Avenue
Denver, CO 80203

CONNECTICUT
State Department of Education
P.O. Box 2219
Hartford, CT 06145

DELAWARE
State Department of Public Instruction
Certification and Personnel Division
Townsend Building
Dover, DE 19901

WASHINGTON, D.C.
Department of Certification and Accreditation
D.C. Public Schools
415 12th Street NW, Room 1004
Washington, DC 20004

FLORIDA
State Department of Education
Capitol Building, PL 116
Tallahassee, FL 32399

GEORGIA
State Department of Education
1622 Twin Towers East
Atlanta, GA 30334

HAWAII
State Department of Education
Office of Personnel Services
P.O. Box 2360
Honolulu, HI 96804

IDAHO
State Department of Education
650 West State Street
Boise, ID 83720

ILLINOIS
State Board of Education
100 North First Street
Springfield, IL 62777

INDIANA
State Department of Education

State House, Room 229
Indianapolis, IN 46204

IOWA
Department of Education
Grimes State Office Building
Des Moines, IA 50319

KANSAS
Kansas State Department of Education
120 East Tenth Street
Topeka, KS 66612

KENTUCKY
Teacher Certification
Kentucky Department of Education
18th Floor, CPT
Frankfort, KY 40601

LOUISIANA
State Department of Education
P.O. Box 44064
Baton Rouge, LA 70804

MAINE
Certification and Placement Division
Department of Educational and Cultural Services
State House Station #23
Augusta, ME 04333

MARYLAND
State Department of Education
200 West Baltimore Street
Baltimore, MD 21201

MASSACHUSETTS
State Department of Education
Quincy Center Plaza
1385 Hancock Street
Quincy, MA 02169

MICHIGAN
Michigan State Department of Education
P.O. Box 30008
Lansing, MI 48909

MINNESOTA
State Department of Education
712 Capitol Square Building
550 Cedar Street
St. Paul, MN 55101

MISSISSIPPI
Office of Teacher Certification
Mississippi Department of Education
P.O. Box 771
Jackson, MS 39205

MISSOURI
Department of Elementary and Secondary Education
Jefferson State Office Building
P.O. Box 480
Jefferson, MO 65102

MONTANA
Office of Public Instruction
State Capitol, Room 106
Helena, MT 59620

NEBRASKA
State Department of Education
P.O. Box 94987
301 Centennial Mall, South
Lincoln, NE 68509

NEVADA
State Department of Education
400 West King Street
Carson City, NV 89710

NEW HAMPSHIRE
State Department of Education
101 Pleasant Street
Concord, NH 03301

NEW JERSEY
State Department of Education
CN 503
225 West State Street
Trenton, NJ 08625

NEW MEXICO
State Department of Education
Education Building
Santa Fe, NM 87501

NEW YORK
State Department of Education
111 Education Building
Albany, NY 12230

NORTH CAROLINA
Department of Public Instruction
116 West Edenton Street
Raleigh, NC 27603

NORTH DAKOTA
State Department of Public Instruction
State Capitol Building, 11th Floor
600 Boulevard Avenue East
Bismarck, ND 58505

OHIO
Ohio State Department of Education
65 South Front Street, Room 808
Columbus, OH 43266

OKLAHOMA
Office of Public Instruction
2500 North Lincoln Boulevard
Oklahoma City, OK 73105

OREGON
Teacher Standards and Practices Commission
State Department of Education
630 Center Street N.E. Suite 200·
Salem, OR 97310

PENNSYLVANIA
Pennsylvania Department of Education
333 Market Street, 10th Floor
Harrisburg, PA 17126

RHODE ISLAND
State Department of Education
22 Hayes Street

Providence, RI 02908

SOUTH CAROLINA
State Department of Education
1429 Senate Street
Columbia, SC 29201

SOUTH DAKOTA
Division of Education
Department of Education and Cultural Affairs
700 Governors Drive
Pierre, SD 57501

TENNESSEE
State Department of Education
100 Cordell Hull Building
Nashville, TN 37219

TEXAS
Texas Education Agency
1701 North Congress Avenue
Austin, TX 78701

UTAH
State Office of Education
250 East 500 South
Salt Lake City, UT 84111

VERMONT
Teacher Certification
State Department of Education
State Office Building
Montpelier, VT 05602

VIRGINIA
Department of Education
P.O. Box 6Q
Richmond, VA 23216

WASHINGTON
Superintendent of Public Instruction
Old Captiol Building, Room FG-11
Olympia, WA 98504

WEST VIRGINIA
State Department of Education

1900 Washington Street
Charleston, WV 25305

WISCONSIN
State Department of Education
125 South Webster Street
Madison, WI 53707

WYOMING
Certification and Accreditation Services Unit
State Department of Education
Hathaway Building
Cheyenne, WY 82002

NATIONAL ORGANIZATIONS FOR PRIVATE SCHOOLS

American Association of Christian Schools
2591 West Beaver Street
Jacksonville, FL 32205

American Montessori Society
150 Fifth Avenue, Suite 203
New York, NY 10011

Association of Christian Schools International
P.O. Box 4097
Whittier, CA 90607

Association of Evangelical Lutheran Churches
Redeemer Lutheran Day School
3212 Ryan Avenue
Philadelphia, PA 19136

Association of Military Colleges and Schools
7009 Arbor Lane
McLean, VA 22101

Christian Day Schools
The American Lutheran Church-DLMC
422 South Fifth Street
Minneapolis, MN 55415

Christian Schools International
3350 East Paris Avenue, S.E.

Grand Rapids, MI 49508

Friends Council on Education
517 Shortridge Drive
Wynnewood, PA 10906

Lutheran Elementary and Secondary Schools
The Lutheran Church-Missouri Synod
1333 South Kirkwood Road
St. Louis, MO 63122

National Association of Episcopal Schools
815 Second Avenue
New York, NY 10017

National Association of Independent Schools
18 Tremont Street
Boston, MA 02108

National Catholic Educational Association
1077 30th Street, N.W., Suite 100
Washington, D.C. 20007

National Society of Hebrew Day Schools
160 Broadway
New York, NY 10038

Seventh-Day Adventist Board of Education, K-12
6840 Eastern Avenue, N.W.
Washington, D.C. 20007

United States Catholic Conference
1312 Massachusetts Avenue, N.W.
Washington, D.C. 20005

United Synagogue Commission on Jewish Education
Solomon Schechter Day School Association
155 Fifth Avenue
New York, NY 10010

RESOURCES FOR SUBSTITUTE TEACHERS

Books

Charles, C.M. *Building Classroom Discipline*. New York: Longman, 1985.
The Commission on Reading. *Becoming a Nation of Readers*. Washington, D.C.: National Institute for Education, 1985.

Glasser, William. *Schools Without Failure*. New York: Harper and Row, 1969.

Goodman, Ken. *What's Whole in Whole Language*. Portsmouth, NH: Heinemann, 1982.

Gordon, Thomas. *T.E.T. Teacher Effectiveness Training*. New York: Wyden, 1974.

Grosswirth, Marvin and Abbie F. Salny. *The Mensa Genius Quiz Book*. Reading, MA: Addison-Wesley, 1981. (and Book 2, 1983)

Hart, Harold H. *Grab a Pencil* series. New York: Hart, 1971.

Koch, Kenneth. *Rose, Where Did You Get that Red?* New York: Random House, 1973.

Pronin, Barbara. *Substitute Teaching*. New York: St. Martin's, 1983.

Smith, Frank. *Reading Without Nonsense*. New York: Teacher's College Press, 1979.

Tchudi, Stephen *et al. Teaching Writing in the Content Areas*. (three booklets: Elementary, Middle School/Junior High, Senior High School) Washington, D.C.: NEA, 1983.

Trelease, Jim. *The Read-Aloud Handbook*. New York: Penguin, 1982.

Virginia Dept. of Education. *Plain Talk About Learning and Writing Across the Curriculum*. Richmond, VA: Commonwealth of Virginia, 1987.

Wylie, C.R. *101 Puzzles in Thought and Logic*. New York: Dover, 1957.

Magazines

Highlights for Children. 2300 W. Fifth Avenue, P.O. Box 269, Columbus, OH 43272

Instructor. 545 Fifth Avenue, New York, NY 10017

Learning. P.O. Box 51588, Boulder, CO 80321-1588

Teaching PreK-8. 325 Post Road West, Westport, CT 06880

INDEX